"*Even the blindest heart could behold the gift of God upon Angie Smith. The messages teeming from her life, her voice, and her pen have the capacity to pierce through all our protective barriers. As she communicates, she throws herself into the same lot with the rest of us who struggle with fears and self-doubts and flaws but she leaves none of us languishing there. God speaks hope, help, and healing through Angie and does it so endearingly and even so humorously that you let your guard down and receive, even before you meant to. I first became acquainted with Angie's story through her blog and remember reading the entire story of her darling baby girl, Audrey, in one sitting. I felt like she was talking straight to me across a small coffee table as she described the heartbreaking news of Audrey's prognosis, the weeks of pregnancy still to come, and the sacred moments they held her in their arms before God swept her into His. She wrote about how Audrey would remain in their hearts forever and, through her story, she has remained in many of ours. Once I got to know more of Angie's journey, I was slack-jawed by the realization that the two of us had our own connection in Christ. The Lord Jesus had called her to salvation as she worked through the Bible study called Breaking Free. What grace to tie two women's lives together with journeys so different by the same woven thread of redemption! He called me to write that journey out of the restoration He brought from my own brokenness. That He would use it to accomplish something so life-giving in her brought me to my knees. I knew her to be a gifted writer as I read her blog, but it was not long before I saw more than that. I saw God blend a natural giftedness for writing with a clear determination to surrender that gift to one gorgeous end: Christ's great fame. And then, I also saw a friend. Angie Smith is a true writer—one who has a perspective that comes only from walking through every shade of life and the shadow of death in His tight grasp.*"

—Beth Moore, Living Proof Ministries

mended

mended

pieces of a life made whole

ANGIE SMITH

Nashville, Tennessee

978-1-4336-7660-4

Published by B&H Publishing Group
Nashville, Tennessee

Dewey Decimal Classification: 248.843
Subject Heading: WOMEN \ CHRISTIAN LIFE \ FAITH

1 2 3 4 5 6 7 8 9 • 16 15 14 13 12

For the Sundays,
who have walked with me through all of these pages.

The Pieces

Introducing *Mended*

If you would have told me fifteen years ago I would be working on a book about my Christian walk, I would have laughed.

And so the story goes, right? God has a way of redefining our expectations.

It has been a labor of love to walk back through some writings published over the past four and a half years on my blog, *Bring the Rain*. The blog began as a way to keep family and friends informed as we walked through the pregnancy of our fourth daughter, Audrey Caroline, who we only got to have with us on this earth for a few short hours. I blogged through the brokenness and hurt, clinging to God's Word and a community emerged. Somewhere along the way I began to consistently get e-mails from people asking if there was some way to combine my more devotionalesque (I'm an author, so I can make up words, right?) entries into book form. *Mended* is the fruit of that vision, and I hope it blesses you and reminds you how loved you are by your Creator. Has something convinced you that you aren't a worthy recipient of His love? Where are the distractions and the noise of life getting in the way of your walk with Him?

Whatever calls our name louder than the voice of Jesus needs to be identified as an obstacle in our walk. Life is busy and days are short. We don't take the time we need to let our souls breathe. I want to invite you into my little corner of the world for a few minutes of your day and ask you to sit with me in the silence. There's no wrong way to read *Mended*. Go at the pace that matches how God is speaking to you. But as you start, let me suggest that you carve a half hour out of the madness each day and let's talk about the way He loves us in spite of ourselves.

My hope is that this will be a resource that leads you to pray and dig deeper into His Word. I have given you some prompts to help with this along the way, whether you are reading alone or with a trusted friend or spouse. Each entry has a focus Scripture, a devotional, and then some brief application ideas. You might need to meditate on one entry longer than another depending on what you are walking through right now, and never feel rushed to move along. I'll be here either way. And most importantly, so will He.

If you are reading *Mended* with someone, I encourage you to have a quick phone/text/e-mail conversation for each entry to help you process your thoughts. I find that when I have this kind of accountability, I tend to make more progress. It doesn't need to be anything spectacular—maybe just a few sentences saying that you need prayer for something or sharing a sentence in the entry that struck you.

There isn't homework and there is no required reading. There are no worksheets, no wrong answers, and no possibility of receiving a failing grade. There is, however, a writer who speaks from her own pieces, and a Savior who speaks from a place of true wholeness.

Invite Him in before you even turn the page.

And if you can hear me whisper above our coffee cups, imagine my smiling face telling you my greatest prayer for you as you read.

The Lord loves you, and He longs for you to have wholeness in Him. In return for your mistakes, He bleeds mercy. In the place of wounds, He gives you this gift . . .

All my love to you, friends.

Be mended.

The Past
and the Pitcher

"Arise, and go down to the potter's house, and there I will let you hear my words." So I went down to the potter's house, and there he was working at his wheel. And the vessel he was making of clay was spoiled in the potter's hand, and he reworked it into another vessel, as it seemed good to the potter to do. Then the word of the LORD came to me: "O house of Israel, can I not do with you as this potter has done? declares the LORD. Behold, like the clay in the potter's hand, so are you in my hand, O house of Israel."

—Jeremiah 18:2–6

 In one of the books I read on grieving the loss of a child, the author suggested smashing a piece of pottery as a form of therapy. When I read that, I thought it was one of the dumbest things I had ever heard.

Then, not long after I read (and dismissed) the idea about smashing a piece of pottery, I was driving along, listening to my favorite worship CD, and talking to God. I try not to dwell on the past any more than I need to, because as with all of us, there are hurts that aren't totally healed.

But, it was a sunny day and I was alone with my music, so I guess it was as good a time as any to remember. As it turns out, I'm glad I did.

Before I get to all that, let me start with my first image of Jesus.

At my grandparents' condo, there was an image of the Lord that hung by the fold-out couch my sister and I used to sleep on in the guest room. It was surrounded by photographs of my dead Italian family, mostly women who: a) looked like they should have slowed down on the lasagna servings, and b) decided collectively that whenever a camera was around, they would pretend they were really angry and stare at the lens. Right there, on the wall of Sicilian terror, hung the face of Christ.

It was one of those "watch you wherever you go" faces. I would wake up in the middle of the night and feel like He was staring at me. I actually devised an elaborate system that involved my sister and me taking shifts so neither of us would be caught unaware in the event that He or any of the dead ladies decided to make a midnight visit.

Let's just say it wasn't a great first impression.

Years later, two events occurred that shaped my life dramatically. The first was during graduate school. My dad called me one day and told me he had been diagnosed with cancer. They were going to do further testing, but things didn't look good. I remember the words *three months* being tossed around. I am a daddy's girl to say the least. Although I had no background with the church, or with the Lord, I decided to do something crazy.

I made a deal with God.

It went something like this: You heal him, and I will find out about You.

It sounds kind of crazy, but I was desperate. The closest thing to prayer I had up to that point was when I asked God in the fifth grade to make my bowl haircut grow out while I slept. He failed me. I have pictures to prove it.

On Christmas Eve we got a phone call from the doctor. The tests had come back.

They couldn't find the cancer.

My family had always been Catholic, so when I got back to the city where I was attending grad school, I called the local Catholic church and asked them how to learn about God. It turned out they had classes for this kind of thing, and they were about to start (go figure). I went to classes for a year and got to know God a little better. I decided I needed to get rid of my boyfriend, whom I had dated for almost six years. He was abusive in every sense of the word, and there are a lot of deep wounds I still carry with me from that time period. It was a completely unhealthy relationship and one of those times I look back on and wish I could change. It hurts because even though I didn't have a relationship with God at the time, I feel like I was unfaithful to Him.

Fast-forward a few years. I was driving home from work and talking to my best friend on the phone. A woman was not paying attention and pulled out right in front of me. I slammed on my brakes but not fast enough to prevent my car from hitting her and rolling over. I remember the sound of glass breaking and a scream (I guess it was mine). I climbed through the window of my Grand Cherokee and cut my shoulder on the way out. It was the only injury I sustained.

I noticed the police officers who came to the scene of the accident were taking pictures of my car, now upside-down in a pool of glass. I asked them why, and they told me that based on the way the car had rolled, coupled with the fact that I wasn't wearing my seat belt, I should have been under the front wheel of the car. I didn't understand why that was interesting enough to photograph until I looked at the car. There was only one item that had come out of the car as I flipped, and it was now pinned under the front wheel. It was the rosary that I had been given by the Church when I finished my classes, and it was covered in my blood. Not a single bead was broken. I knew in that moment what many people are blessed enough to learn early in life.

He died for me.

Later that night I went to the chapel with my best friend (after she came flying to the hospital with wet hair because she had heard the wreck happen while we were on the phone), and we cried together at His mercy. The door started to open for a relationship with Christ, but I didn't fully let Him in.

All of that was about to change. I had become friends with some Christians who were really trying to get me into the whole church world. They invited me on a retreat thing, and to be honest, I thought that pulling my arm hair out sounded like more fun, but I was desperate.

The theme of the retreat was grace. I walked by a room where the group leading worship was rehearsing, and I saw him. The man who became my husband. He loves this story, because I basically fell head-over-heels for him instantly. I have my journal entry from that day, and this is what I wrote:

> *"Lord, I know I'm not good enough for him. But could you just let me have someone like him?"*

Almost eleven years and five kids later, I am a better person because God let me have him.

So, back to the pottery and the drive to the airport. As I was driving, God spoke to me clearly, and He asked me to do something odd. I started thinking about a certain pitcher I have in my house, and as soon as it came to mind, He told me to smash it. I thought about that book that said to break a piece of pottery and how I had kind of shrugged it off, but I really felt like that's what God wanted me to do. Thankfully, my neighbors know me well enough to not call the police when I throw a perfectly good pitcher onto my front porch at ten o'clock at night. I watched it shatter, and I must apologize to the author of that book for my initial skepticism. It felt great.

I waited for a few moments, taking it in. What next? I asked.

Again, He was very clear.

Put it back together again.

What I wanted to do was go to bed, but I felt like He was meaning *now*, so I gathered all the pieces together and brought them in the house. I told Todd what was going on, and he took a look at the tiny shards of porcelain, knowing it was going to be a long night. I went and got the hot glue gun and sat down in the kitchen. It was hard to know where to start, but I found the lip and the handle relatively intact, and just kind of made it up as I went. I talked to the Lord while my fingers worked, and He stayed near to me. I would love to tell you that it was like a movie where everything about the moment was all sweet and perfect, but the truth is that I glued my finger to it at one point and cut myself several times. I thought about swear words that I wanted to say. But, still I kept at it.

And as I worked, He let me think about my past. Mistakes I have long regretted. I began to realize that this pitcher was my life, and every piece was part of a story that He had chosen to put together. I started crying, and remembering things I thought I had forgotten. It took a long time to finish, but it was time well spent. Every nook and cranny whispered to me, until at last it stood in all its imperfection.

Here you are, Angie. You are mended. You are filled with My Spirit, and I am asking you to pour yourself out.

The image of my life as a broken pitcher was beautiful to me, but at the same time, it was hard to look at all of the cracks. I ran my fingers along them and told Him I wished it had been different. I wished I had always loved Him, always obeyed Him, always sought Him the way I should. I was mad at the imperfections, years wasted, gaping holes where it should be smooth.

But God, my ever-gracious God, was gentle and yet convicting as He explained.

My dearest Angie. How do you think the world has seen Me? If it wasn't for the cracks, I couldn't seep out the way I do. I chose the pitcher. I chose you, just as you are.

At the risk of sounding like a nutcase, I am going to make a suggestion. Find a piece of pottery, and let it shatter at your feet. Then take the time to be with the Lord as you piece it together again (but beware the wrath of the glue gun!). Let Him tell you who you are, and let yourself be reminded of the grace that seals us all. You may not know Him at all, or you may be a "flannel-board Jesus" kid. It makes no difference. As I type these words I am praying that He will come to you and remind you that He loves the gaps because there is the potential for more of Himself to be revealed in you. Let Him help you smash and rebuild His most coveted possession . . . you.

mending

— I'm willing to bet that you have seasons of your life that feel "unmendable." Despite the heartache you have over the choices you have made, it's never too late for Him to sculpt you into something beautiful. Consider a time when you were not walking with Him the way you would like to have been. What were the circumstances? How can you protect yourself from walking there again? Spend some time today praying through your thought process as you look back. Allow the Lord to remind you that you aren't a mistake. I'm big on list making, so sometimes it helps me to write down things that made me susceptible to making bad choices. I have found that it doesn't normally happen out of nowhere, but is a combination of factors. The more I identify the factors, the easier it is to see when I'm starting to drift again.

— I want you to have a "pottery" experience of your own. Find a (preferably cheap!) piece of pottery that you can break. It can be a bowl, a vase, a pitcher, or anything that will give the same effect. I learned the hard way that it would have been easier to put it in a plastic bag before I dropped it (let's just say the kids had to wear shoes for several weeks on that porch to avoid wayward shards!). Break the pottery, and glue it back together. Take your time; it isn't a race. It's an opportunity for the Lord to speak to you, and for you to be reminded of His great love for you—His precious broken vessel.

— Whether here, in a journal, or on a Post-it note, write one word, thought, or prayer that came to mind as you read "The Past and the Pitcher." Continue this with every entry throughout *Mended* and pray that God will remind you of what He showed you in these entries whenever you hear or think of those words as you go about life.

Your Road to Emmaus

When he was at table with them, he took the bread and blessed and broke it and gave it to them. And their eyes were opened, and they recognized him. And he vanished from their sight. They said to each other, "Did not our hearts burn within us while he talked to us on the road, while he opened to us the Scriptures?"

—Luke 24:30–32

 I always loved the idea of God, but He just didn't seem practical, and for most of my life, "not practical" meant "not necessary." I put my full weight into what I could see and touch, and I found out the hard way that this life let me down (several times). I tried to read the Bible, but it just seemed huge and totally foreign to me. I felt like it had nothing to do with my life. I decided to read it the whole way through before I made up my mind, but I only got a few chapters into Genesis and decided it was less fun than trigonometry. I hosted a Young Life group in my basement in high school, but truth be told, it was because there were some really cute Christian boys whom I wanted to notice me (it didn't work . . . turns out they really were coming over for Jesus). I used to sit on my bed and say "Show me you're real!" to God

and then let my Bible fall open, pointing my finger randomly at the page, positive He was going to give me a Scripture that would answer all of my nagging questions. He taught me two great lessons in my "Bible-pointing" days.

1. I can't put God in a box, and I cannot expect Him to show up on my timetable.
2. I pretty much always end up somewhere in 1 or 2 Chronicles, wondering why God loves the word *begat* so much.

Years ago, I sat down with my Bible and I asked the Lord to speak. Unlike the other times, I wasn't "testing" Him; I just wanted to feel His presence with me. By this time I knew Him, and that definitely changed my attitude and motives as I sought Him in the pages. I didn't do it because I wanted Him to prove anything, but rather because I was hungry for Him. He led me to two stories within a matter of days, the first being the story of the Lord calling Samuel (1 Sam. 3:1–21). It is still one of my favorites, and includes what was, for me, the key that began to turn the door of faith: "Speak, LORD, your servant is listening" (v. 10 NLT). It has become something I repeat over and over as I go about my daily life. I realized that God had created me to be in communication with Him. He wanted me to invite Him into corners of my life that seemed too small for Him to fit. I began to listen, and I invited Him to speak.

The other story is in the Gospel of Luke, where two people are traveling the road to Emmaus. I decided I was going to read it over and over again, slowly digesting the words and asking God to reveal Himself to me. I did a little word study and found that the name *Emmaus* means "warm springs," and that these springs were frequently used for healing purposes. So I began to picture two people walking toward "healing" instead of to just some random biblical location. The full story is found in Luke 24:13–32, but here is the gist of what is captured in that passage.

Three days after Christ was crucified, two of His disciples were walking to Emmaus, and they were sad because they didn't feel convinced that He was risen, or that He was really the Christ at all. They were discussing this when a man (Jesus, raised from the dead) "catches up" to them. The word used is the Greek word *eggizo,* which means "to draw near, approach."

The men didn't know who He was. They told Him all about their disappointment, sharing that they had believed Jesus was the promised One, but now they doubted. There was no evidence.

There they were, walking with the living Christ, and they had no idea who He was. They were looking past His face and into the abyss that demands proof. They saw His sandals, His hair, His eyes, His robe, but they did not see Him. They continued walking side by side for miles as He spoke to them, reminding them of everything from Moses to the prophets, but they did not know their Shepherd.

Finally, they reached their destination. Jesus acted as if He was going to continue on, but they begged Him to stay for supper. They longed to be in His company, so they invited Him to be their guest. As they sat around the table, their eyes were opened. Scripture says that Jesus "took the bread and blessed and broke it and gave it to them. And their eyes were opened, and they recognized him" (vv. 30–31). Immediately upon their recognition, He disappeared from their sight, and they asked each other, "Did not our hearts burn within us while he talked to us on the road, while he opened to us the Scriptures?" (v. 32). It all finally made sense. He was the great Rescuer. They immediately headed to Jerusalem to share their news. "We have seen Him! He is risen!"

I realized that in this beautiful story, God had posed a very important question to me, and He may be asking you the same.

Where are you on the road to Emmaus?

I thought about the way I had finally slowed down enough so He could catch up to me. I thought about how I had walked for years beside Him but never really knew who He was. Then I thought about the way I was drawn to Him and how I had invited Him to stay with me. And then, the bread was broken, and I saw Him for who He is.

Just as the disciples said, I remembered the way my heart had burned for Him, even before my eyes were opened. I love the Greek word that is used to communicate how the disciples felt as they walked with Him, not recognizing who He was. It is *kaio*, and it means "to set on fire, to be consumed."

This has crystallized in a way for me, and has helped me understand the walk of the believer in a tangible way. I write this knowing that we are all in different places along our walk with the living Christ, but there are some things each of us can do, no matter where we are.

1. Walk slowly and deliberately with thoughts of Him on your mind. He will catch up.
2. Listen when He speaks. You will want to be with Him longer.
3. Invite Him to stay. He will accept.
4. Acknowledge who He is when He reveals Himself to you. He is Jesus Christ, the son of God. He was crucified, and paid the full penalty for sin. He died on the cross and was resurrected on the third day. He is now in heaven, where all those who trust in Him will spend eternity with Him. If you've not truly acknowledged Him before, do so now. Confess your need for Him,

your complete dependence upon His sacrifice to pay the penalty for your sins. Acknowledge your trust in Him to save and keep you.

5. Allow yourself to be consumed with love for Him.

I hope more than anything that this book encourages you to open your Bible and ask the Lord to reveal Himself in His words. Ask Him to make it come alive for you as you read. Before you begin, say a prayer asking Him to slow you down and help you focus on the words. Sometimes I just read the same sentence over and over until I feel like I am ready to move on to the next. I had to get past my "speed reader" tendencies and see Scripture for what it was . . . God's letter of love to us, His workmanship.

Have a blessed day. It is the day He has made. He knows the plans He has for you today and every day. Each thing you will face and each need you will have. If you have never believed in Him before, I am praying that today is the day of broken bread.

Speak, Lord. Your servants are listening.

mending

— Have you ever had an experience when you felt certain the Lord was speaking to you? Many people say they have not, so don't feel like you're in the minority if you haven't had such a moment. What I think is so interesting about this particular Bible story is that Christ's disciples didn't even recognize His voice until later, when He allowed them to do so. It was only then, in looking back, that they recognized what had happened. In my own life I can think of times I felt a nudge to do something (or not!) only to later reflect on that time and realize that I should have listened to what was (I believe) the Lord speaking to me. Pray that you will become more sensitive to His voice in your everyday walk, and that you will recognize when He is asking you to do something.

— Throughout the day today, pause in busy moments and remind yourself that you need only to be consumed by Him. Not the carpool line, the endless to-do list, the dishes, or whatever is distracting you. Ask Him specifically to focus your mind on Him, and ask Him to make Himself bigger in that moment than everything around you. Enjoy this sweet Emmaus, friend.

CRUCIFIED BY LOVE

I have been crucified with Christ. It is no longer I that live, but Christ who lives in me. And the life I now live in the flesh I live by faith in the Son of God, who loved me and gave himself for me.

—GALATIANS 2:20–21

 The Lord spoke to me just about a year after the loss of our daughter, Audrey, as I was reading my daughters the story of Jesus' crucifixion. I was reading from their children's Bible, which recalls the stories of the Bible beautifully. Part of the way through reading the story aloud, I literally stopped midsentence and had to compose myself because the words were breathtaking. Here is an excerpt from The Jesus Storybook Bible:

> *They nailed Jesus to the cross.*
> *"Father, forgive them," Jesus gasped. "They don't under-*
> *stand what they are doing."*
> *"You say you have come to rescue us!" people shouted.*
> *"But you can't even rescue yourself!"*
> *But they were wrong. Jesus could have rescued himself. A*
> *legion of angels would have flown to his side—if he'd called.*

*"If you were really the Son of God, you could just climb
down off that cross!" they said.
And of course they were right. Jesus could have just
climbed down. Actually, he could have just said a word and
made it all stop. Like when he healed the little girl. And
stilled the storm. And fed 5000 people.
But Jesus stayed.
You see, they didn't understand. It wasn't the nails that
kept Jesus there.
It was love.*[1]

For some reason, I hadn't quite thought it through in those terms, and I was rendered speechless by the infinite power that was denied for the sake of love. This is, for me, one of the simplest and most powerful ways to present the gospel, even stretching into our lives today.

Why do you choose to be crucified with Christ? You have the choice to abandon it all. Just walk away and say that this road is too hard. You need a break. You aren't strong enough to withstand the pain of the nails.

Suddenly it was very clear to me that it has never been the nails that held me here. It has been love. It has been a deep, desperate, longing love for the One Who was mocked on my behalf. The One Who I rejected for sin's fleeting pleasures.

As I sought to walk with God through the loss of my daughter, I realized that since the day I first heard His name, I had two choices: be crucified with Him, or climb down.

I have felt the sting of death deeply, and there has never been the option to walk away. Not because I couldn't, but rather, because I was blessed in the most unexpected way to invite the nails that held me to Him.

It is as if He is saying, *"Sweet child. The nails are not enough to hold you here. You can only live the life I am calling you to through the love I have given you. The love that now has taken up residence in your very being and makes the wounds bearable . . ."*

He beckons each of us to nestle deep into the brokenness and find inexplicable comfort. He woos us to touch His bleeding side so we will know that we are not alone. I can tell you that I have done this, and I have been rescued from a pit so deep I could not fathom a way out of it. You may be down there right now, begging for mercy and for relief.

We who are followers of the King must daily wake up and look in the mirror, seeing our reflection with a crown of thorns balanced on our heads. We must feel the burden of the cross at different points in our life. In the power of Christ, we will look back solemnly at ourselves and say, "I am choosing to bear the crown because I cannot live without the love."

That's easy to say, isn't it? Will you trust me enough to try it? Tell Him, the One who knows your deepest fears and most secret desperation, that you are choosing the thorns.

Every day.

And one day, not so far from now, I believe we will be made complete, and pain will cease completely.

Oh, Lord, come quickly.

But until then, make your life an offering, and allow the hands of the Father to carry you through what you think is impossible.

I assure you that through it, He will show you His boundless, freeing love, which allows us the strength to make it another day. And another day. And then, one glorious day, He will call for us.

I can't prove it to you, but I know it deep, deep within myself.

The stone has been moved.

He is risen.

And I love Him, even in the excruciating pain I feel. If you are trying to pursue relationship out of forced conviction, you will miss out on the glory of falling in love with the Maker of your soul.

There is such a difference between religion and relationship. I could not have survived without the latter, I assure you. Because, you see, the thing about the nails in this life is that they are temporary. We choose to bear them because we know that we will lay our crowns at His feet in the blink of an eye. We will join Him for eternity, and will worship the One Who was scarred on our behalf.

I am praying for each of you as you walk in His love today and arise tomorrow morning. I am praying that you will see the crown of thorns as a promise. Yes, it is painful, and yes, sometimes we struggle under the weight of it, but no, it will not defeat us. It isn't something superhuman or overly spiritual, just the daily remembrance of a life lived out of the depths of love.

We praise Your name, Lord. For You are who You say You are. And that is enough.

mending

— If you're anything like me (or most of my friends), you have trouble believing that God could love YOU this way. You might feel like there is something hidden in you that would repulse everyone around you, or a secret thought that haunts you. The mere thought Jesus knows it is enough to make you feel unworthy. For many people, this could be the deal breaker between dragging your feet in bondage and walking in the fullness of freedom. Or perhaps you are a "do-er" and struggle with believing that you could be loved apart from somehow earning it. It might not be easy to believe, but it's true. He loves you. Three words that, fully appreciated, have the power to set your life on fire for Him. Meditate on what is holding you back from believing it, and spend today praying that He would remove those barriers and lead you deeper into His heart for you.

WHY WEREN'T YOU MOSES?

*For consider your calling, brothers: not many of you were wise
according to worldly standards, not many were powerful, not many
were of noble birth. But God chose what is foolish in the world to
shame the wise; God chose what is weak in the world to shame the
strong; God chose what is low and despised in the world, even things
that are not, to bring to nothing things that are, so that no human
being might boast in the presence of God. And because of him you are
in Christ Jesus, who became to us wisdom from God, righteousness
and sanctification and redemption, so that, as it is written, "Let the
one who boasts, boast in the Lord."*

—1 CORINTHIANS 1:26–31

 Our family was on a road trip when I decided
to download *Chasing Francis: A Pilgrim's Tale*, a
book I have wanted to read for quite a while. A
few chapters in I realized I was using the "high-
lighting" function more than I typically do. I
decided Todd would enjoy it as much as I was. I read out loud for
a few paragraphs, slowing to make sure I was making notes of my
favorite parts, and then I trailed off as I realized I had probably
overestimated his desire to have me read the book to him.

Apparently I was wrong, and Todd asked me to keep going. An hour and a half later we were wrapped up in the story, hushing the little ones while they sang from the backseat because we were so eager to hear what happened next. They, of course, thought this was hilarious, so Justin Bieber was the background music for our book. Solid.

There were pages that made me pause because I had to have space to process the profundity of the idea. It's told so beautifully that you are knee deep in a story of a man, but also a centuries-old follower of Christ. I have long been fascinated by the life of Saint Francis of Assisi, but I could not have anticipated what I would glean from the story portion of the book. In one section, the following conversation takes place:

> *"Do you know the story of Rabbi Zusya?" he asked.*
> *"He was a Chasidic master who lived in the 1700s.*
> *One day he said, "When I get to the heavenly court,*
> *God will not ask me, Why weren't you Moses?"*
> *Rather he will ask me, "Why were you not Zusya?"*[2]

The man speaking let that thought hang in the air for a moment, then continued.

> *"Churches should be places where people come to hear the*
> *story of God and to tell their own. That's how we find out*
> *how the two relate. Tell your story with all of its shadows*
> *and fog, so people can understand their own. They want a*
> *leader who's authentic, someone trying to figure out how to*
> *follow the Lord Jesus in the joy and wreckage of life. They*
> *need you, not Moses," he said.*[3]

Wow.
They need you.

Not Moses.

I don't know who your "Moses" is, but I can think of several people in my life whom I have seen myself as such a pale shadow of—people I look up to and want to emulate in some sense. At the heart of it, it isn't even what I see as greatness in them, but rather the way it casts light on the weaknesses I perceive in myself. How much time do I spend comparing, contrasting, evaluating, doubting, and allowing myself to feel like a disappointment when the Lord tells me over and over that He loves me?

There will be no measuring stick when we see our Savior face to face. I have images of apologizing to Him, fumbling for words as I have tried (no better than a toddling child) to convince Him that I want to be as good as "so and so" or as brave as "so and so."

I am realizing more and more that I am not in charge of how I compare to anyone else. I need not look at my failings and others' successes, imagining that I have failed the Lord or disappointed Him. What a waste it is to watch each other and long for what others have, how they manage to do it all so well, and why in the world we can't get our act together enough to be as good at having a quiet time or so ruthlessly capable of memorizing Scripture. Did I think there was going to be a "verse-off" with another soul entering heaven when my name is called? Maybe I would have to do a little Bible map work, or prove I could put the books of both the Old and New Testament in order?

How wildly ridiculous, right? Then why is it, sister, that we spend our days doing exactly this?

May we all hear the words so truly spoken in this amazing story, and may the message soak you with truth that permeates your insecurities, your doubts, and your misgivings about what you have to offer. Thank God for you, just as you are. God doesn't want you to be Moses, friend. He wants you to be you loving Him.

You aren't Moses (or whomever you put in his place), and you won't be. God wouldn't have it any other way. May the peace of that gentle reminder fall on you, and may it secure something in you that may have been rattling around, determined to find a satisfactory answer.

Face what is before you with confidence and with a heart aligned with the One who knew your name before time began. He sings songs over you and quiets you with His love (Zeph. 3:17). If you are brave enough to listen, you might hear the sound of your own name echoing back from the great I AM.

Jesus, we praise You for the provision to create each of us as distinct, precious, holy images of You, and we ask Your blessing over us. Help us to love each other well, encourage each other to the heights, listen until there are no more words, chasten only when mandated, and appreciate all things unique. And most of all, Lord, thank You for the mighty work You are doing in each one of us every single day. Amen.

mending

— Why do we do this?!?!?! Oh, it's awful. The comparison game . . . are you stuck in it? Do you look at everyone around you and wish you had a fraction of their _____ (fill in the blank)? To a certain degree I believe we all do this, but a lot of us pretend we don't. I think it's best to just look this thing in the face and acknowledge it. Most of us aren't going to wake up every day and smile at our amazing selves in the mirror, thinking, "Wow, Lord. I don't see how I could possibly get better." But what we can do is shut down the voice of the enemy as soon as we hear it, not allowing the lies to send us into unnecessary battles. We don't get to see ourselves the way the Lord sees us, but we can choose to believe what He says about us. In fact, I doubt He's real keen on us wishing away all the things that He designed. Where are the places you deal with this the most? Your mirror? Your kids' school? The gym? The office? Create a tangible reminder that will help you nip these thoughts in the bud. It might be as simple as a Post-it note or as detailed as a bracelet with a word that will remind you to compare yourself only to Christ, recognizing that He has made the provision for us to be seen just as He is. Give yourself a reminder of this, something that you can direct your focus to and go straight to Him instead of following those thoughts any further.

THE SCARLET CORD

May the God of peace, who through the blood of the eternal covenant brought back from the dead our Lord Jesus, that great Shepherd of the sheep, equip you with everything good for doing his will, and may he work in us what is pleasing to him, through Jesus Christ, to whom be the glory for ever and ever. Amen.

—Hebrews 13:20–21

 Her name was Rahab, and she was a prostitute. I must say, she is one of my favorite heroines in Scripture. In the event that you don't know her story, find a cozy chair and flip to the second chapter of Joshua. First, let me give you a little background on where we are in the Bible when we come to the story of Rahab. Moses had died without ever entering the Promised Land and his successor was the mighty warrior Joshua. Joshua was planning to invade Canaan, and in order to scope out the land, he sent in two spies. We don't know their names, but we do know that they were told to focus on Jericho. While they were there, the spies stayed at the home of a prostitute named Rahab. It has been speculated that they chose this location because it was unlikely that they would be discovered in a brothel. One way or another, by the

end of their time there, they had changed the course of her life, and in a sense, all of our lives.

The king of Jericho received word that there were spies in the land, and he sent his representatives to Rahab's house. Instead of turning them in, she lied to them and told them that the spies had been there, but had left and were on their way out of the city. While the guards rushed through the night streets, Rahab crawled up to her roof where she had hidden the men under stalks of flax. She whispered to them and told them that she knew what the Lord had done for them. She had heard about the parting of the sea, and she believed that God Himself was on their side. She told them that she believed their God is "God in the heavens above and on the earth beneath" (Josh. 2:11). Essentially, she believed in God more than she feared for herself. She lied to the authorities to protect these strangers because she wanted to be on the side of God, as they were.

She told the spies that she would keep them safe as long as they promised not to harm her family when they stormed the city. They agreed. She let down a cord from her window and helped them with an escape plan out of the city. The men told her that they would be back to battle shortly, and in order for her family to be kept safe, she must do one thing. She was to gather her family into her home and then drop a scarlet cord from her window to signify that they were to be spared in the fighting.

It wasn't the first time the Lord used a symbol like this, foreshadowing the blood shed by Christ. Remember when Moses was trying to convince Pharoah to let his people go, and a series of tragic plagues swept the land as he refused to release them? During the last plague, God told Moses that unless a family had taken the blood of a lamb and put it on the sides and the tops of their doorframes, their first-born sons would die in the night. The houses with the blood on them would be "passed over (hence the holiday Passover)," and the children would live.

The blood of a lamb . . . the scarlet cord . . . the cross at Calvary . . .

This is one of the things I love most about my Jesus. He is the God of redemption. He loves to take the underdog and show them that they are not who they thought they were. He took a woman living a sinful life and He blessed her because she believed in God with holy, reverent fear. He didn't just "let" her into the story. He chose her for the story.

He chose you for the story.

The story of Rahab brings tears of gratitude to my eyes. The blood-red cord comes spilling from a window, desperately clutched on one end by a woman who believes in the God she has yet to meet. This is the cord that will save her and her family from disaster.

So where are we in all of this? We are the sinners who have the power of the scarlet cord, dropped in faith and held with utter conviction that He will save us.

I don't always love my Lord the way I want to. I get distracted, my mind wanders, my fingers become busy, Old Navy has a clearance sale . . . oh, I get off task easily . . .

I have something I like to do when I feel like I am wandering from Him, drifting just a little bit (or maybe a whole lot). It has been one of the most powerful exercises I have done during my life as a Christian, and it never fails to move me to tears. I find a comfortable place (usually my bed), and I get settled. I take a moment to just be still. This is a challenge in itself most days, but when I do it, I know that it is because He is going to make Himself known to me in the next few moments. I close my eyes, and the first thing I imagine is the crown of thorns, cutting into His sweet, bloody brow. I look at the crown. In my mind, I run my fingers gently across the thorns and I whisper to Him. I just sit in the sorrow for a bit, and when I feel ready, I let my mind's eye travel to His face and His beaten body. His arms, aching from being stretched out and held up. I spend time studying His sunken cheeks, His hollowed eyes, His chest, His arms, and oh, Lord, His wrists. The blood that came from a nail, spilled for me . . . I gradually see His back, beaten beyond human recognition. I move slowly, taking it all in. I trace the wounds; I weep with Him. I thank Him. I see His legs, hung weightlessly into the base of the cross, nails driven through his ankles. I imagine what it must have felt like as the nails pierced His skin. I hear the shouting, the chaos, the overwhelming sense that the moment of death is near. I am another woman who stands at the foot of the cross, forgiven. I am another woman clinging to the scarlet rope.

And here is the best part of the story, and probably the least expected twist in the plot. At some later point in time, Rahab becomes pregnant, and gives birth to a son, whom she names "Boaz" (see Matt. 1:5). Remember Boaz? You may recall that he was symbolic of Christ as the "kinsmen redeemer" who married Ruth in the book of Ruth. Are you ready for this family tree?

Rahab is the mother of Boaz.

Boaz is the father of Obed.

Obed is the father of Jessie

Jessie is the father of David.

Let's skip a couple of generations and see where we end up . . .

. . . and Jacob the father of Joseph, the husband of Mary, of whom was born Jesus, who is called Christ.

She was a sin-filled woman with a controversial story.

She was a castoff.

She was imperfect, immoral, improper.

She was hand-picked to be part of His lineage.

She was redeemed by faith.

Twelve years ago, I opened a window and dropped a scarlet cord.

And my Lord, despite my hardships, has kept His promises to me. One day I will stand before Him and I will see the wounds with my own eyes. I will thank Him. I will bow down low, and I will worship the One who wore the crown of redemption. I will spend eternity in a place where there is no more hurt. A place where my sweet Audrey waits for me. I cannot wait for that moment. I want to see Him, to love Him, to adore the One who saved me.

And maybe, just maybe, there will be a giant closeout at Old Navy up there . . .

mending

— Isn't it reassuring to be reminded that God can use sin-damaged people to bring Him glory? I can never hear it enough. In the event that you're with me on this one, I'm going to ask you a hard question. You can answer it quickly and scoot on to the next reading, or you can process it slowly and see what comes to you. Either way, don't miss the opportunity, because there's great healing in addressing this struggle. Here goes: *What is the thing from your past that you fear will keep you from God?*

— I can think of a couple of situations/people/experiences that once held me in bondage in this way. It grieves me to remember. If you are a believer in Christ, He paid the price for whatever you answered to this question. You might not ever forget it, but the truth is this: It doesn't separate you from Him.

— Commit to giving voice to this struggle in whatever way you feel comfortable. You may not want to go into detail with the person to whom you have chosen to confess this struggle, whether that is a spouse, friend, or small group, but there is great value in the encouragement and accountability that comes from sharing that with which we struggle with other believers. The enemy would love for you to be swallowed by your guilt and shame, and there is power in being reminded it isn't so with Jesus.

FLEE AND DON'T LOOK BACK

Not that I have already obtained this or am already perfect, but I press on to make it my own, because Christ Jesus has made me his own. Brothers, I do not consider that I have made it my own. But one thing I do: forgetting what lies behind and straining forward to what lies ahead, I press on toward the goal for the prize of the upward call of God in Christ Jesus.

—PHILIPPIANS 3:12–14

 I sat completely upright, eyes staring at him while I moved food around my plate nervously. It was our first date, and I had decided I was going to marry him. He ordered (delicious) soup for me and opened the car door when I got in and when I got out. I wanted to impress him, but I choked on my words as I tried to come up with something less desperate than "Elope or have a wedding?"

Because that's not always a good first-date plan.

His eyes lit up as he shared a story he had heard about a little girl at church who had drawn a picture, and he just knew I would get a kick out of it as well.

"So, you know Lot's wife?"

Clearly Lot was a friend I hadn't met yet. I put on my best "I'm sure I do . . . give me a minute . . ." face and nodded for him to continue. Was that the guy in Sunday school? Was he on the retreat? Lot. No, I would remember meeting a guy named Lot.

"Well, her teacher told her to draw a picture of what happened to Lot's wife, and she drew a salt shaker."

He started laughing. I laughed, too, and shook my head side to side. Those crazy kids.

"Oh, that is great! How funny." I bit my lip and tried to think of a good follow-up condiment story.

Nothing.

"So, Lot . . ." I just kind of threw it out there. I figured I would give him some room to fill me in on the backstory.

"Yeah, you know, from Genesis? The one who left Sodom and Gomorrah?"

Awesome. Thanks for clearing that up. Note to self: find *Precious Moments Bible* that is somewhere in my apartment and find out who Sodom and Gomorrah are.

I nodded again, filling my mouth with pasta so I wouldn't have to drop any more pearls of wisdom before the second date.

A few hours later I found my little Bible and hunted down this Lot guy. He's umm, an interesting fellow, and reading about him next to images of Precious Moments figurines has got to be one of the strangest experiences a new believer can have.

With that said, it really is an incredible story. It's a little odd to me that it's so often used as one of the typical children's Bible stories, but if you look at it through the lens of an adult, it is incredible.

God told Abraham that if there were ten righteous men in Sodom, He would not destroy the city. Unfortunately, there were not ten righteous men to be found, so God sent two angels to warn

Abraham and his nephew Lot to get out of town. Lot tried to warn his sons-in-law, but they thought he was joking and apparently didn't listen. It says in Genesis 19:16 that Lot hesitated, so the angels grabbed his and his wife's hands along with their daughters and led them out of the city.

As soon as they were safe, the angels said to them, "Flee for your lives! Don't look back, and don't stop anywhere in the plain! Flee to the mountains or you will be swept away!" (Gen. 19:17 HCSB). Yet, Lot tells them he wants to go to another town instead. And guess what? It isn't in the mountains; it's in the plains. God wants Lot to go to one place, but he believes his idea is better than God's. I read this and shook my head because that just sounded silly to me.

Well, as silly as it can sound to someone who does the same thing almost every day of her life.

God grants Lot permission to go to the nearby town instead of the mountains, telling them to hurry. So Lot, his wife, and their daughters head toward the nearby town. As they do, Lot's wife makes a critical mistake.

She looks back.

She looks back at the city filled with sin and wickedness, and as she pauses, God turns her into a pillar of salt (the salt shaker thing is way funnier now).

We don't ever learn her name, but her legacy is one of looking back. She has been rescued from death, from sin and depravity, and there is something that still haunts her enough to stop her from moving toward whatever is ahead. Did she want to see if it would really be ruined? Maybe she wanted to see her things one more time. Was she longing for a person? Or reflecting on the life she wanted to keep living?

I don't know, but I do know this: God has been gracious to me for many years as I have exercised a tendency to look back.

A glimpse of what could have been. A temptation that makes me question my faith. An earth-shattering loss that beckons me to believe that the mountain is too far and the valley will be just fine.

I have wandered to the closest city while I know He desires for me to climb—and I have settled there for longer than I care to remember. I have failed Him many times over, head and heart turned, and yet He urges me never to settle. I don't know what you are walking away from as you read this, but as I have been praying about what to write, the Lord has put this message on my heart so clearly that I had to share it. I want you to know I am praying for you as I write—asking the Lord to remind you right now that there is a reason you have left that life behind.

It has been swallowed by grace. And you need not miss what He has for you by believing there is something worth going back for. Leave it be. The Lord has told you where to go, and it's time to walk. Eyes straight ahead, tangled in the spectacular love of a Savior Who wants nothing less for you than the summit. And when you stare at what might have been, you are immobilized, unable to bring Him the glory He deserves. And also, He might make you salt. Just saying.

When this book releases, it will be right at twelve years from that first date with Todd. October 2012 will mark twelve years of falling in love with the man who has given me five daughters and many, many more dates. No matter how many times we sit together over a meal, I will never forget the first one. It was a night that turned out to be a heart-fluttering, life-altering, dream-come-true night when I learned about a woman who loved in the wrong direction.

I still get confused about Bible references. I am the farthest thing from a Bible scholar. I can't tell you the Hebrew and Greek roots of all the words, nor every battle of the Bible or city mentioned in Scripture. What I am confidently saying is actually pretty simple.

He is who He says He is, and He is whispering if you care to listen . . .

"Flee, love. Flee and never look back."

mending

— There is such a long road behind us. As much as we fight it, there is often the temptation to remember it differently from what it really was. Do you ever rewrite history? Look back fondly on something and then come up empty when you try to recreate it in the present? If there was a season of sin in your past that you remember with any fondness, you can be sure Satan wants to keep it dressed up in its fancy clothes. You might even start to think you had it better then and get caught up in wishing you could go back there. I believe that when Lot's wife looked back, it was more than just a casual encounter. I think she wanted to live in the place she knew was wretched, and no matter what God had revealed to her, she was determined to desire it. Where do you have the tendency to do this?

— God's Word is one of the greatest tools we have. It is especially helpful when breaking patterns of sin or struggle. Memorize Philippians 3:12–14 and ask the Lord to help you model what it teaches.

Honeysuckles and Fireflies

For we are his workmanship, created in Christ Jesus for good works,
which God prepared beforehand, that we should walk in them.

—Ephesians 2:10

The first time I saw him was at dusk on the kind of summer day that makes Southerners whisper, "I'll be," while fanning their necks with whatever they can get their hands on. Needless to say, I was on my way inside when his silhouette caught my eye. I turned just in time to see him motioning to someone else while his pitcher's glove hung at his side. He looked to be a teenager from my vantage point, but I didn't look long enough to know for sure. I had things melting in my grocery bags and air conditioning whispering my name while the crickets started their night songs.

I closed the door, pulled the curtains until they met in the middle of the back door, and figured I would introduce myself to the boy in the common area behind my house another day. Surely there would be a cooler day when I could be friendly, right?

A few days later I was on my way to a play date and I could see him from the back again. He had his mitt and was wearing a jersey that looked more like a winter choice than mid-July cloth-ing. I could hear him yelling into the distance at what I presumed to be the same friend, and I made a quick waving motion in their direction in an attempt to look friendly as I got into my car. As I reversed out of my driveway, I paused, and as I watched his arms move wildly, I wondered how in the world someone could be verti-cal in this heat, let alone moving.

Three hours later we pulled back into the driveway, and I squinted through the trees to make sure my eyes weren't playing tricks on me.

He hadn't moved.

His jersey was soaked through with sweat; his hair was sopping wet as he wiped his face with the back of his mitt-free arm.

"Is that . . . ?" I stared straight ahead, convinced I must be imagining it.

"Those boys are always playing out there, Mommy." Ellie shook her head and unbuckled herself, eyeing the door, and then in a swift, deliberate motion she burst it open and made a dash for the house.

I looked in the rearview mirror at Abby.

"Honey, have you met that boy yet? Does he play on the high school team?

Abby shook her head no and raised and lowered her shoulders, fingers on the door handle.

I carefully took Charlotte out of her car seat and watched him out of the corner of my eye. All of a sudden he shouted, and I jerked her awake by accident. She was just a few months old at the time and had that newborn, panicked cry as I grabbed the rest of my bags and made my way inside.

He never turned around.

I walked into the house and told Todd that the boys were

playing again and that I was going to go introduce myself to them. I handed the baby over, grabbed a couple of bottled waters, and went outside.

Sometime in the span of those three minutes, he had completely disappeared from view. I sat on my back steps for a few more minutes and then gave up.

After all, it was hot.

By the time August rolled into our new neighborhood, we had gotten to know some of the other kids, and one day while they were swinging outside, I asked the little girl who lives across the street who the boy was.

"Oh, that's Andrew," she replied nonchalantly. "But he's not really a boy. I mean, he's close to his twenties, I think." She sipped her drink and tucked her flyaway hair back under her hat.

"Really? Because every time I see him he's playing baseball with someone else, and he screams loud and points all around, and I can't tell what . . ."

"Oh, Ms. Angie, he isn't playing with anyone else," she interrupted. "He's done that for years."

She watched my eyes squint in confusion and offered up an answer before I could ask.

"He has Down syndrome. He just loves to pretend, I think." She smiled.

I closed my eyes for a moment as I tried to retrace the outlines I had seen in the evenings, and I realized that I hadn't actually seen another person playing. I had presumed there was someone else because of his screaming, but there never was another voice.

I looked at her and nodded. The girls ran off to play, and I put Charlotte in a little bouncer seat in the shade while hoping he would come back out so I could meet him. He didn't come out that day, nor the next. In fact, almost three weeks passed until one day

I was upstairs cleaning, and I heard the familiar sound of a player urging his players to round the bases.

I ran outside, barefooted on the gravel, and started to walk towards him.

I took a few steps and stopped, sensing that it wasn't time for me to speak. Without taking my eyes off him, I lowered myself onto the little brick half-wall around our porch as he raised his hands high in the air and shouted. It was clear that the game had gone his way, and as he waved to all the fans and made a victory lap, I was mesmerized.

My sundress was sticking to my back as the gnats made a mess of my legs. I tucked them underneath me, scraping them along the ragged brick as I craned my neck to see what was going to happen next.

It was at this point that I noticed that although he always had a mitt, I had never seen either a ball or a bat. I smiled as I realized he didn't need them. He had everything he needed for the perfect game.

Something to receive the imaginary ball. The voice to thank his adoring fans. The persistence of a seasoned ballplayer on a hot summer day. And last, but not least, the ability to see the whole thing in a way I never could. Because on that night, and dozens more since then, I have seen the same thing happen. A man-boy with a leather glove and a field of fireflies believes he is victorious.

I have never spoken to him. In fact, I don't even know his last name. As many times as I have watched him play, I have yet to even see his face. My house sits behind the catcher, I suppose. There isn't much need to turn away from the field. As much as I would love to shake his hand and tell him the joy he has brought me, I have the sense that my back porch is close enough for his comfort.

I have prayed for him many times, and I've asked the Lord to grant me a version of what he has, because I realize I am woefully unable to dedicate myself to anything the way he has devoted himself to the game.

The game.

How do I play it?

Well, first off, I run away from the heat.

Also, I wouldn't dare play without a proper bat and regulation-sized baseball.

I would have real bases, real fans, and also, real prize money.

And I wonder if I would bother to play at all if nobody was watching.

Yet day after day, season after season, the same boy in the same jersey with the same dedication takes his place on the field.

Why?

Well, I suppose it's because winning isn't really found in any of the things he's missing. More than that, I'll tell you this: in a solid year of living here, I have yet to see him lose a game. He cheers, he runs, he takes grandiose bows in front of an empty field while we shuffle our groceries and our children and our dreams in and out of the car, in and out of the house, in and out of, well, life.

It was a mild October afternoon when I realized I didn't ever need to see him to love him. I had started to learn some of his motions and what they meant, and one day before the sun fell down, I heard him call out into the silence.

"Bring 'em in! Bring 'em in! Come on! Run! RUN! RUN!!!!." He was waving wildly and I was sitting with a book on a blanket in the backyard. I tried to peek through the slats in the fence, but he moved just out of sight. I jumped to my feet and while I have no idea what possessed me, I just got so excited that I lost track of monitoring my responses. His voice hit a fevered pitch, and I felt my fingers tighten around the top of the fence, waiting in eager anticipation for what would happen next.

I swear to you that just for a brief moment, I saw what he saw.

There were runners on the bases, coaches in a frenzy, and a crowd on the edge of their seats. The ball dropped, the men ran, and the boy made me believe. He threw his glove on the ground and started jumping up and down and clapping, and before I knew it, I let out a holler like I had just won the lottery. I knocked over my Diet Coke and covered my mouth out of fear that I would scare him. I didn't. In fact, he never knew I was there.

I made a promise to myself that I have been intentional about remembering when the days get long and the heat is oppressive. It doesn't matter who is watching. It doesn't matter what you think you can bring to the game.

What God needs from you is the sweat rolling down your neck and a heart that believes He can use you.

Every time the air starts to smell like honeysuckle and the fireflies dance through the trees, I peek out the window, hoping to catch a glimpse of the boy who taught me how to love the game. I pray this is the season of life in which you see the glory of God through the lens of a boy who plays like he can't lose.

Soak every bit of it up, even if it means your ice cream melts or your task list suffers.

Because before you know it, the leaves on this season will be falling, and it will be too late. You have exactly what you need right now, and more than that, you have a God who stands perched while waiting to round you home.

Take your place, friends.

It's time to play ball.

mending

— What do you admire about someone else's relationship with the Lord? This isn't meant to beat you down or get you caught in the comparison game, but rather to inspire you. There's a difference, and it's all in what it leads you to pursue. Here's an example. There's a girl I know who has a fantastic marriage. They seem to get along all the time, and they're just so loving with one another. If I think about it during a time when Todd and I are in one of the normal struggles that come in all marriages, it would be easy for me to go the wrong way and think, "What's wrong with me?" or "I'm so jealous this isn't what I have." But, the same situation could also lead me to productive, God-honoring thoughts, "Lord, help me be the kind of woman that has that patience and view of life." Or "Inspire me to love Todd as a true reflection of You."

— Now's the chance for you to think about a person whom you really look up to spiritually and evaluate what it is you appreciate. Is it discipline? Then let's focus on that and come up with some ideas on how to grow in that area. Maybe joy? Okay then. Let the Lord inspire you to walk closer to Him . . . and feel free to look to those around you as long as what you're really seeing is how He is working in them.

Us, Not Me

Do nothing from selfish ambition or conceit, but in humility count others more significant than yourselves.

—Philippians 2:3

 The first time I met author and speaker Beth Moore, she was wearing her pajamas, she had on no makeup, and she had rollers in her hair. Before you call the police, she had actually invited me to her hotel room. In the span of just a few minutes, she said a couple of things that will always stick with me, and one of those was this sentence:

"Angie, I want you to know I esteem you."

This isn't a bragging session about me, I assure you. It is actually quite the opposite, and it comes with a challenge for us all. Several months later, I heard her speak at an event where she made a point of discussing the way we are to be praying for one another as sisters in Christ. She had generations of women stand and pray for each other, and it was unbelievably powerful. Eight thousand women lifted one another up to the Lord and acknowledged the gift that each particular generation was.

The heart of her message pricked my heart so deeply that it has defined the way I pray for women in ministry. As I started to pray after the message, I felt the Lord bring several women to mind, and I have started a list of their names. On more than one occasion I realized that they were women who could be seen by the world as "competition" to me.

Hear me say this very clearly, because I don't want *this* to be misread. I don't think I'm some hotshot who needs to be concerned with keeping up and being on top of the pack. I think it's quite possible that when I get to see the Lord face-to-face I will only be able to stammer, "Why on earth did You ever trust someone like me to do what You allowed me to do?" That isn't false humility; it is knowledge of myself and the complete conviction that I am a beautiful mess of grace and flesh. It is only by His will that I walk on any platform or plunk out any words for people to read.

And may it always be so.

In my heart I recognize the peace that comes from knowing I have no desire to stake a claim as if it were my own to stake. It isn't because of the ministry to which God has called me that I do this, but because I am a daughter of the King who believed in the power of humility and the impact His submission had on those around Him.

Maybe while you were reading this, several people came to mind, like women from a playgroup, work, Bible study, social interactions, or anywhere else there would be the potential for you to feel threatened in your role or insignificant in your own skin. I firmly believe Satan gets a major foothold when he convinces us that we have people we need to keep up with, when that voice in the back of your head whispers, "That promotion should have been yours," or, "If you invite her to this event, everyone will just forget about you," or maybe even something like, "There's only room for one, and if you help her up it will leave you in the dust."

There is no competition, ladies. There is no little room that only a few can enter.

There are two choices, and the ironic part is that they don't affect the other person the way they affect you.

Start right now, and do something bold. Ask God to humble you and raise others up. If that last sentence made you bristle, chances are the Lord desires this to be a place that is fully surrendered to Him, and we can assume that this nudge is from the Holy Spirit. We need to hear encouragement from other sisters in the Lord, and they need to hear them from us. We need to stop believing that these words of affirmation do anything to jeopardize our own standing.

It can be someone you respect, admire, or any other number of things, but before the sun sets on this day, reach out and tell that person that she means something to you, and make a commitment in your heart to pray that God will use her.

I can't help but wonder what it would look like if this became a habit among Christian women and it took the world by storm. Wouldn't it be great if people would say, "Oh, those Christian women, boy do they know how to love one another!"?

What do you say? Pen in your hand or fingers on the keyboard, take a few minutes and do the thing I'm asking the Lord to inspire you to.

Go ahead.

Show everyone what true, Jesus-filled love looks like. Who knows? It might catch on.

mending

— Sometimes it is easy to be kind and encouraging—
other times it is more of an uphill battle. Given the strong-
hold that comparison and jealousy can be, this might be
one of those more difficult ones for you. But we have been
called to be humble as Christ was humble and to love one
another so the world might know we are His. So, let's bear
down and follow through on what I mentioned above.
Reach out with an e-mail or phone call to a woman whom
God is using. Affirm her and commit to pray for her.

— Scripture teaches us that God looks to our heart and
that He loves a humble heart. He will use you, but His
power through you will be all the greater if you are serving
with a humble heart. Pray today asking Him to humble
you and raise others up. Be honest with Him about any
struggles with jealousy, and ask Him to give you a loving,
grateful heart.

The Sea and the Scarf

Are not two sparrows sold for a penny? And not one of them will fall
to the ground apart from your Father.

—Matthew 10:29

I was reminded of one of my father-in-law's favorite stories to tell about my kids, and it happened to take place while we were on a cruise. I was still pregnant with Audrey, and we knew her diagnosis. We had committed as a family to go on a cruise where Selah would be singing and ultimately decided we needed to keep that commitment despite what was happening with my pregnancy. I was nervous about people's reactions to me, obviously pregnant, but with a child that many knew we didn't expect to bring home. It was actually a much nicer time than I had gotten myself all worried about, and people were very kind to me. Women would just sit by me at the pool and ask about the book I was reading, and then eventually transition into a story about loss in their own lives.

This particular story involves my sweet Ellie, who was five at the time. We were out on an excursion in a smaller fishing boat. She was mesmerized by the way you could see the "fish" swimming below us (let me clarify that "seaweed" and "fish" are seen as equally exciting to a preschooler). It was a rusty, nasty fishing boat, and the "activity director" decided it would be more productive to flirt with the captain, so we were left to explore the wonders of not-what-we-hoped-for-ville by ourselves.

I would have been even madder about the less-than-ideal boat conditions if my daughter hadn't said something that I carry with me every day of my life. There was a woman aboard the ship who was battling cancer. She usually wore some kind of hat or scarf, and for formal events she donned a beautiful wig, but the girls were concerned when they saw her at the pool one day and asked me what was wrong.

I told them that she had something called "cancer," that we needed to pray for her because it makes her very sick, and that the medicine she was taking made all of her hair fall out. They stared at me in confusion, which made me want to tell them that everything was going to be fine, but that would have been a lie. I didn't know enough of her story to say what was going to happen, only that we should pray for the woman with the scarves. And every night, in earnest, we sat on our little cruise-ship bed and talked about our prayers. Inevitably, the "special scarf lady" made her way into their requests. I can't tell you that they fully understood what might happen to her, but they were lifting her up as if they did.

I should preface this next part of the story by saying that Abby and Ellie don't let people into their world very easily. They have each other and they have us, and that's about all they need. If you were to meet them, they would most likely hide behind me and stare at the ground while Kate busts in front of me, introduces herself and proceeds to ask you to pick her up and carry her around like you're a horsey, yelling "GIDDY UP!!!!" until you have reached sufficient canter.

Todd and I have an interesting combination of genes.

All that to say, Abby and Ellie aren't fond of strangers. So when we boarded the little excursion boat and saw the scarf lady, I knew they were going to be nervous. But guess where Ellie sidled up? You guessed it. Right in between her grandfather and the scarf lady. I almost passed out.

I couldn't hear the conversation over the loud motor, but at one point I saw Ellie talking to the woman, and I was mesmerized by the look in her eyes. It reminded me of myself, and it was a side I had never seen in her before. She wasn't intimidated. She wanted to connect with her.

And in that little five-year-old face, I didn't see panic or even sadness, but just a simple empathy that belied her age. I watched them pointing at things and talking about what they were seeing, but I couldn't make out their words. At one point, Ellie pointed at her scarf. I found out later that she told her she knew why she wore it and that we had been praying for her. I can't say for sure, but I have a feeling that if we all could be this bold as adults, the world would be a different place.

In Beth Moore's Bible study *Esther*, she talks about the way we want to separate ourselves from those who are in pain because we fear it may overtake us as well.[4] It is human nature to want to fix things; I know because I am the worst of all. I hate seeing people suffer, and will do anything to make it go away.

The problem is that sometimes you can't.

As the ride continued, Ellie and the scarf lady kept talking. I still didn't know what all they were talking about, but at one point I saw Ellie get very serious and start pointing at all of the things around. She would point, and then look at the lady as if making sure she understood. Then, she would do the same, this time with her eyes on the sky or the coastline. The woman was nodding and looking at her with love.

Ellie paused for a long while, silently staring out at the seemingly endless waters, and then turned to face her sweet friend. I couldn't hear what she said, but the woman and my father-in-law both threw their heads back in laughter. I was really curious about what had transpired because it was so out of character, but I was even more concerned that I was going to be sick from the lack of stability on the rust-ridden boat, so I buried my head for the rest of the trip.

When we got off the boat on a little island, I asked my father-in-law what Ellie had been saying.

Ellie started by telling the woman that she liked her with her hair or without it and that she thought her scarves were pretty. She proceeded to ask her if she knew that God was a big God who could do big things. The woman nodded sweetly.

Ellie then started pointing at the waves and said, "See? God's hands made those waves."

Then she looked up at the sky and told the woman, "God made the blue sky, the huge blue sky and all of the birds and clouds."

She proceeded to inform her that God's hands made all of the sand on the shore and all the fish in the sea.

This continued for some time, and then there was the pause.

I asked my father-in-law what she had said that had made them laugh so hard, and he said that she had turned to the woman and said, "I think He did make all of these things, but I don't think He can make a peanut butter and jelly sandwich."

I laughed and kissed her wet, sandy head as we headed off for the beach. I told her that I was proud of her for making a new friend. She smiled as she responded, "Yeah, she thought I was funny."

As I sat and watched the girls play in the water, I thought more and more about what she said, and it has since become a very profound part of my journey with God.

I have no doubt that His hands, His HUGE hands make the sky and the earth and the planets and the stars and so on and so on.

But is it possible that those same hands can wrap themselves around something as small as a knife? Something so small as my day-to-day needs? My hurts? My fears and doubts? The situations that seem like nothing to those around me but keep me awake at night?

He can make the waters part. No problem. That makes sense to me. BIG hands. Got it.

He can resurrect His dead Son from a cross. He is God after all.

But can—and does—He wrap those same hands around the "little things?"

The divorce papers that I have seen filed to friends? The bills that friends can't pay? The e-mails I get every day asking for prayer for sick family members, dying babies, husbands at war . . .

I don't know that Ellie had any idea what she was really communicating; I do believe the Holy Spirit allowed her to minister to a stranger from a place that we, as adult Christians, are sometimes afraid to enter into.

It is the place where it's easier to talk about the sand than the cancer.

It's easier to talk about the glory of His great hands that weave global Kingdom plans than face that you have no hair and no guarantees in this life.

Are there places in your life where you think, "God wouldn't care about this. He's got too much on His plate to try and figure out how to help me through this day."

May I be honest? Sometimes I do.

As much as I trust in Him, believe He is Who He says He is,

and welcome the opportunity to praise Him, there are moments when I think I might have fallen off His radar because He is busy, you know, saving the world and all.

I feel like a tiny, tiny peanut butter sandwich, and it is hard to picture His hands on the tiny knife.

I know it isn't biblical. I have dozens of Scriptures that tell me that. Can I just say this, though? As someone who loves and trusts Him more that I could ever articulate?

It doesn't always feel that way.

So instead of giving you the pretty Christian answer of what IS true, I am going to give you the human "Angie answer."

It doesn't always feel that way.

Where are you spiritually? What is it in your life that challenges your trust in His steady hand? There is nothing too small for Him to care about. I am praying (for you and for me) that we open our eyes to the truth. There is unspeakable beauty in the work of the Master's hands, and I don't want to miss a moment of it. Whether it is by boldly considering what is under the scarf or by faithfully knowing His great hand can manage the tiniest of knives, I am praying for His ever-present love to surround you.

God bless you, and may the peace of God settle deep within you. Even in the little things.

mending

— What is it in your life that feels like it could be insignificant to God? Even though we know how He loves us, it is tempting to think that aspects of our lives aren't "God-worthy." We just don't have the ability to understand His capacity for love. He doesn't stand still and choose the place in the universe that needs His attention the most. He is omniscient, omnipresent, omnipotent. Three big words that really just mean He is able to love you everywhere, all the time, and with all power. He will love you in a way you have never been loved, whether it's in the caverns of life or just in steadying the knife on a peanut butter and jelly sandwich. Spend some time talking to the Lord about the little things, trusting Him to provide for you.

— Is there or has there been a person in your life who has made you feel insignificant? I've heard it said many times that a woman looks to her father as an earthly model of her heavenly Father. If you had or have a difficult relationship with him, it's easy to see that there could be an impact on your faith. Maybe it wasn't your dad but someone else who made you feel like you weren't worthy of love. Perhaps it's a relationship that you're still in. Make today a day when you give that pain to Jesus and ask Him for a divine transfer. Ask Him to reveal Himself to you as a loving, providing Father. Consider sharing this struggle with your spouse or a trusted friend, asking for prayer support as you seek to lean into what it means to trust the Lord and all that He says about His care for you.

The Glorious Hem

He will wipe every tear from their eyes, and death shall be no more,
neither shall there be mourning, nor crying, nor pain anymore, for
the former things have passed away. And he who was seated on the
throne said, "Behold, I am making all things new." Also he said,
"Write this down, for these words are trustworthy and true."

—Revelation 21:4–5

So, it was spring. Thus, Todd and I decided to do some spring-cleaning. I was excited about most of the plans, but there was one project I was absolutely dreading—cleaning out our closets. I was dreading it for a few reasons, not the least of which was that there were some sassy pants in a size 2 that I knew needed to be surrendered to the "in your dreams" pile. I was also dreading cleaning out the girl's closets because there were stacks of clothes that needed to be sorted by size and season, and different piles for people who have little girls. I had been putting it off forever, but I finally committed to the task, set up shop, and started reaching for the piles.

About a half hour later, I was in tears. I hadn't expected it to be so mentally draining. If you're a mom, you may know exactly what was getting at me. I really feel like I view life as photographs. I remembered the outfit Ellie was wearing when she realized that the hose water was freezing and about two seconds later when she taught Abby the same lesson the hard way. I remembered what Kate wore home from the hospital and in what blankie I first photographed her. I remembered the bathing suit Abby was wearing when she felt beach sand for the first time. I remembered the dresses the girls were wearing the preceding Christmas, when I was a few months pregnant with a baby girl I thought was healthy.

As I made my way into my closet, I felt so heavy with sadness. I started throwing my maternity clothes into a giant bag while I had a little "conversation" with God. It was pretty one-sided.

At least it was at first.

After a few minutes, I looked up and saw the bag that has my wedding dress in it. In that moment, I felt a prompting from the Lord that I needed to unzip the bag. It seemed a little odd, but I know Him well enough to know that I should just obey the urging and let Him guide me to where I am supposed to be. I unzipped the bag, and for a brief moment, my mind was consumed with the fact that I used to have a 21-inch waist. Then I remembered that the God of the Universe was speaking to me, so I returned to a posture of listening.

I pulled the bottom of the dress out of the bag and the train came spilling out. I spread it out on the ground and studied it as moments of my wedding day came to mind. I started to relax, and my eyes drifted to the edges of the train. And I saw the most incredible, unexpected thing.

The hem of my gown is dirty. *Really dirty.*

I know how it got that way. I walked down a church aisle, took photographs in the grass, and danced and ate my way to happiness. I lived in it.

A few dresses down from my wedding gown is the dress I wore when we buried Audrey. It is dirty as well, but not from happiness. It is stained with fresh earth, wrinkled from kneeling by my daughter's grave.

And so I sat on my closet floor asking the Lord to show me why He had brought me here. I closed my eyes and imagined the hem of my wedding gown as I danced with my new husband.

"And I saw the holy city, new Jerusalem, coming down out of heaven from God, prepared as a bride adorned for her husband" (Rev. 21:2).

I couldn't remember that whole passage as I sat in the floor of the closet, but the words "You are the bride of Christ" came to mind. I suddenly pictured the image of myself in a glorious white gown that floated all around me, a seemingly endless train chasing after me as I walked.

And then, Him.

I couldn't see Him in my mind, but I felt a great peace as I imagined my hands clutching at fabric all around me so I could run to where He was. I imagined myself falling before Him as my dirty gown settled all around me. Dirty from my sin. Dirty from the hurt and the disappointment. Dirty from dancing in joy. Dirty from years of walking across a wet graveyard. Dirty from loving deeply, richly, completely. Dirty from the fears, the dreams, the sorrow, the confusion. Dirty from the memories, the regrets, the mistakes, the injustice of this world.

Stained by this life, I have walked while my Savior whispered, "One day I will wipe your tears, my sweet bride . . ."

What a glorious hem surrounds us all. It follows us wherever we go, gathering up pieces of this life in anticipation of the next.

One day, I will bow to the King of Kings, and I will worship Him.

And as He wipes the tears from my eyes, I will ask Him the question that cannot be answered fully from a closet floor . . . *Where is she, Lord?*

In the meantime, I will start to think of my days like a wedding photograph. I will walk, veiled, down this long aisle, in breathless anticipation of the day that awaits me.

I will trust in the One Who will make all things new in His time.

I will keep my eyes on Him Who waits for me.

I will.

Or rather, I do.

mending

— I love memories from my wedding day. It was such a day of peace and genuine excitement for the life we had ahead of ourselves. Then, a few weeks after we were married, the September 11th terrorist attacks occurred. Todd was on the road (in D.C.), and I was on my way to work when I got the news. I was a new bride in a world where everything felt upside down. Every channel flashed horrific images, and I desperately wanted Todd to be with me so we could comfort each other. It isn't so different with us and the Lord. This life is chaos, and although we know that we are His bride, sometimes it feels like we will never get to Him. Another building, another life, another loss. It can feel like too much to trust in the great Hope that waits for us in eternity. It's hard to comprehend that such a beautiful Savior would want a bride like me, but it's true. There is nothing that can separate Him from those who are His. Do you believe that today? Where do the areas in your life where you could walk with a firmer step to the end of the aisle? Where are the pockets of doubt creep up? Bring those to the Lord today, and envision yourself as exactly what you are: the magnificent object of His great and enduring love.

Worth More Than Diamonds

*Thus says the LORD: "Let not the wise man boast in his wisdom,
let not the mighty man boast in his might, let not the rich man boast
in his riches, but let him who boasts boast in this,
that he understands and knows me, that I am the LORD who
practices steadfast love, justice, and righteousness in the earth.
For in these things I delight, declares the LORD."*

—JEREMIAH 9:23–24

 Kate was concerned that our guest wasn't wearing a wedding ring. "Is she married or not married?" she asked in a whisper. Well, it was a whisper for Kate. Which means that everyone in the room was now paying attention. Nikki giggled and answered in her thick Australian accent.

"Yes, I am married, but I don't usually wear my ring. It's very special, though." Kate nodded like she didn't believe her. She was five, and when you're five, you play by the rules. The rules say no ring means the marriage isn't legit. I waited until Kate went to bed and then I asked Nikki about it, because there was something in her voice that made me think there was a story hiding in there somewhere.

"It's actually a really amazing story," she started out. I was already sold on the story because of the way her voice lilted up at the end like she was asking me a question. She began clicking away on the keyboard of my computer and I saw her pull up some pictures online. She spun the laptop around to face me when she found the page she was looking for, and there was absolutely no way I was going to hide my, umm, enthusiasm. I planned to say something along the lines of "Oh that's just lovely" and maybe make my voice get higher so she would feel at home with me. But it came out more elegant, like, "Oh my WORD!!!! That is HUGE!!!"

No lilt. No shame. Just a girl who was face-to-the-screen with a diamond the size of a state. She giggled. I'm going to go out on a limb and say she had seen my googly-eyed look before. Without even needing to be asked, she began to tell the story.

"So, my grandfather used to mine stones in Australia. He owned a piece of land there, and this particular stone has quite a history." I leaned in to listen and ultimately realized I was acting creeptastic and staring at her, so I backed up. Play it cool. Yeah, that lasted all of four seconds. She smiled as I unashamedly motioned my hands in a forward motion to urge her on.

"He mined this stone, and when my mother was thirteen years old, he let her cut a stone with him. It was hard work, you know, because you cut a diamond with another diamond, and you just have to keep doing it until it gets all the facets you want it to have." Actually, I didn't know. But I shook my head because creeptastic was back in town, and what in the world could be cooler than a girl talking about a mystery diamond. Oh wait, I know. A girl who sounds like Nicole Kidman talking about a mystery diamond.

"And this was the one they cut together. The very first one she ever cut with her father. She wore it for my whole life, until I got married. Then we had it put in another setting, and now it's mine."

She smiled and looked back at the screen. It was a sweet story, and that would have been enough for me to make a few phone calls and see if we could get a Lifetime movie in the works, but she wasn't finished yet.

"Can I ask a rude question?" I said, and then I realize that whenever you phrase a sentence this way, you have already asked a rude question and really there is no going back. But, she was so friendly and open that I knew she was going to answer without being offended, so I dug right in and asked how many carats it was. I mean, burning minds want to know. The other guests in the room got quiet and started to listen. They had been wondering themselves, I'm sure. And the door was open. Come on crew, let's walk on in.

"I actually have no idea. That's kind of part of the mystery of the stone. I actually don't even know for sure that it's a diamond." She kept talking about some other cool stone it might be, but I had already skipped ahead in my mind to this great jeweler we know. I was making mental notes about setting her up for a little appraisal because I think it's going to be an oh-happy-day kind of experience, but I'm jarred by the end of her thought.

". . . and I made a promise that I would never find out."

I looked at her with my mouth hanging open, and I was tongue-tied about where to go from there because who in the world has a wedding ring that her mother has worn for her entire life and she can't find out what it is?

I'll tell you who.

Nikki, the Australian girl.

She knew I wouldn't be able to form sentences because this was too good to be true.

"So here's the story."

"My grandfather wanted to teach my mother a valuable lesson

about the difference between value and worth. So as they cut this stone together, he made her promise she would never find out what its worldly value is. He told her that it wasn't the amount of money it could fetch, but rather the fact that it had worth. He had mined it on his own land and they had cut it together. That was what gave it worth-not the dollar amount."

You could have heard a pin drop. I needed to come up with something spectacular to say in that moment, because how often do you hear a story THIS good?

"SHUT. UP." Classy. That's all I have to say about that.

"No, seriously. So I have honored that promise, and I'll never take it to a jeweler or anyone to find out. Isn't that neat?"

I did make a fool out of myself by asking about four million questions after that, which led me to later kick myself for not acting more poised and reserved about the whole thing.

It's been weeks since I sat with Nikki upstairs in my house while the television blared the latest headlines and I hung on her every word. I don't remember much about the other things we discussed, but I do remember the spectacular lesson she gave me on the beauty of worth.

So many times in this life, we are convinced that it is money, recognition, approval, accolades, or degrees that give us credibility and will make us feel like we've made it. It's easy to fall into the trap, because let's face it, the world loves the shine. I get it. I mean, I GET it.

But what if we had something that was so precious that we didn't even let the world tell us what it was worth?

We would protect it, keep it close, and pray that it would always be ours, wouldn't we? This is how I want to think of my walk with Christ . . . like this stone. I can torment myself over the questions I have, the doubts I feel sometimes, the genuine curiosity about my life. But instead of spending my days chasing after answers, I have realized that I have something much more beautiful.

I have the stone.

Given to me as a gift I never could have earned. Worn proudly by His bride, those who trust in Him. Cut at great cost, over and over again until the sun fell down and the curtain was torn in two.

For me.

For you.

Oh, precious One.

May I be a reflection of Your great worth all the days that You give me.

mending

– We so often confuse worth and value in this crazy life. We click a button, write a check (if anyone other than me even still does that), and try to buy our way to happiness. It's so easy to depend on your earthy possessions to identify worth, when the truth is, most of the time our "stuff" is swallowing us alive. We are a society that is drunk from entitlement and oblivious to who the Lord says we are. If we could see things from His perspective, I have a feeling we would shudder at the amount we have allowed our view of Him to be clouded by our desire for more, more, more. Do you look to things of worldly value to bring you worth? Be specific as you think through this area of potential bondage. Ask the Lord to give you a clear vision of what it is you need to surrender in order to understand your worth through His eyes instead of everyone else's. Confess this area of struggle to your spouse or a trusted friend and ask for accountability and encouragement as you seek to focus more wholly on the Lord. I daresay you won't want to look much farther than Him once you catch a glimpse of the way He sees you. You are worth so much more than sparrows, and His plan always included you. You don't need to buy your way in or impress anyone to claim it. He is yours and you are His. Allow that mercy to soak deep into your skin-deep life today.

WICKED WEEDS

So then, brothers, we are debtors, not to the flesh, to live according to
the flesh. For if you live according to the flesh you will die,
but if by the Spirit you put to death the deeds of the body,
you will live. For all who are led by the Spirit of God are sons
of God. For you did not receive the spirit of slavery to fall back into
fear, but you have received the Spirit of adoption as sons,
by whom we cry, "Abba! Father!"

—ROMANS 8:12–15

It was hotter than it should have been for that day as my daughter and I were evaluating the state of our lawn. We walked hand in hand, barefoot in the tall grass, and I bent down to pull up a weed. Ellie looked at me with an expression of outrage that belied her age.

"Mommy, why you pull that up?"

"Because it's a weed, honey."

My fingers reached over and over again into the warm earth as my thoughts drifted elsewhere. I thought about what I was going to make for dinner, what time I needed to wake up the baby, where my lost car keys could have gone, and many other seemingly important questions. I felt a tug at the back of my shirt and shifted my focus.

"Hi, Ellie. What do you need, honey?"

"What's a weed?" The curious blue eyes were searching me, waiting for an answer that would clarify why Mommy was tearing up the yard that Daddy had been working so hard on that summer.

"Oh, baby, a weed is not a good thing. It is going to try and kill all of our grass." I tried to read Ellie's face to see if this explanation satisfied her. I imagined it would. At the tender age of three and a half, she had already become my rule-enforcer, my child of justice, the one who always pointed out the color of upcoming traffic lights as we drove and corrected children on the playground for using "potty talk."

Her eyes widened and she crouched down, eye to eye with the killer weeds. An air of righteousness overtook her as she said in her sternest voice, "Oh dear. You are trying to kill grass. Naughty, naughty." Ellie tipped her chin back to look at me, the sun flooding her face, and she smiled the smile that meant "I took care of it."

I patted her fiery red head. "Thanks, Ellie. Now run along and play." I watched as she dusted the dirt cautiously from her knees and shifted her hair out of her face. As she started walking toward her twin sister, she announced, "Abby, those weeds are trying to kill something. We gotta get 'em!"

Abby, more similar to Ellie in looks than moral reasoning, turned briefly and gave a supportive horrified look to show Ellie she had heard the news. Then she went back to drinking water from the sprinkler while doing what looked to be a choreographed frenzy of joy.

The next day, Ellie approached me while I was sitting in the yard watching the sun set in the trees behind our house. My heart was heavy with the gravity of daily life, and as she always did, Ellie sensed that something was not right.

"Mommy, why you feeling that?" Ellie's choice of words took me off guard; I myself was unable to identify the "that" in what I was feeling.

Her tiny, sweaty hand ran along my arm, and I looked into a deep place in her, replying gently, "Today Mommy is feeling kind of down. It's all right; Mommy is okay. Just thinking about things."

I didn't want Ellie to feel my burden, so instead of letting my thoughts get the better of me, I began to tickle her and roll her around in the hot grass. A look of shock came over her, and I pulled my arms back, trying to imagine what could have upset her.

"Baby, are you okay? Did Mommy hurt you?" Ellie's eyes were looking over my head, and I tried to follow her gaze.

"No. I think I see a wicked. I gonna get it." Hands on hips, she walked a few steps from where we were, her tiny sneakers carving a path of determination. She lowered her body deliberately and pointed at a weed that was towering over the grass.

"Look." She turned to see what effect her discovery would have on me. Assured that I had seen the problem, she clarified her concern. "Is that a wicked or a grass?"

Where she heard the word *wicked* in reference to a weed, I don't know, but I do know that there was great importance in the elimination of the correct green species in our yard. God forbid she should pull up a piece of healthy grass!

What a funny little girl, I thought, and then I realized something. To the three-year-old eye, and maybe even to the thirty-year-old eye, weeds and grass look very similar. Same color, same feeling, same texture. In fact, I realized that the "wicked" and the grass were only discernibly different to me because I had seen them for enough years to know the difference. I looked down into red cheeks and pursed lips.

"That's a weed." Ellie gave a nod of supportive confirmation and turned toward the little green enemy.

"Hmm. You tryin' to kill something?" she interrogated the weed, either out of a sense of power over it or a sense of unease about what was to come next. Ellie looked at me one more time, waiting for me to tell her, as I do several times each day, that this was not a good choice. My silence must have been translated as permission, and she reached, gently, to touch the weed. But instead of pulling the whole thing out, she touched the tiny leaves of the "wicked" and pulled it just enough to remove a sliver. She discarded it quickly and reached in for more. I watched as she did this several times, not at all put out by the fact that she appeared to be doing very little to stop the killer weeds that were threatening our grass as we knew it.

It was at this moment, as I sat beside her in the grass, that I realized God was teaching me more than proper lawn care. I thought about how many times, even in a day, I reach to pull the "wicked" one leaf at a time, and all the while it is growing bigger and stronger all around me. I am seasoned enough in my walk to identify the weeds in my life, and I am much too tentative when it comes to removing them.

I sat and stared at my Ellie, so much like her mommy in so many ways, as she delicately plucked leaf from leaf. I wanted her to learn more from the moment, as I had, and so I put my fingers around hers, noticing that we both had dirt under our fingernails. I moved her hands away and took firm grip on the base of the weed.

"Here, let me show you." I jiggled it as I went to make sure the root came up with the weed. Side to side, delicately at first, and then when I sensed it would come up in one whole piece, I tugged it out in one quick motion.

Ellie marveled at the long roots dangling down and the gap left in our ground.

"See how Mommy got the whole thing? You want me to help you learn?" Ellie nodded and I pointed to another weed a few feet away. She rose confidently and approached the "wicked" with a new realization: *I know your secret.*

We spent the next hour walking side by side, saying very little, rejoicing in the holes that were cropping up all over Daddy's lawn. For both of us, there was a sense that they were a small price to pay for the greater good.

We both got better as we went along, learning the way different weeds come up out of the dirt. Some are long and skinny, and those just take one good pull. Others are leafy and the roots are stubborn. Sometimes you have to dig all around the weed and tug gently. We became a great team.

As the waning sun looked down on us that Thursday night, I learned something about the boldness we should claim in approaching our sin. We kneel, we face it eye to eye, we clarify that it is not of our Lord, and then, in utter confidence, we grasp it by its strongest point and destroy it. We don't have to do it alone, and we don't have to do it in fear.

We are tended to by the great gardener Himself, whose deepest longings are met as we walk in the joy of gaping holes that He can pour Himself into and raise life anew.

I pray that you learn to be bold with the sins you face in your life, not as one who fears the gardening, but as one whose desire is to be blameless and pure as you sense the Father beckoning you to rid your life of weeds (Phil. 2:15).

mending

— I would like to plead a lack of knowledge and say that most of the time I don't really know the difference between the wicked weeds and the good grass, but the truth is, I often do. Whether or not I protect the weeds isn't a matter of just recognizing the weed for what it is, but possessing the conviction to grab hold of the roots and yank like my life depends on it. I sit captivated as a friend teases someone, and I laugh instead of expressing disapproval. I listen to gossip and perhaps even pass it along. I complain bitterly about my husband to a friend and say that I just needed to "vent." I'm guessing that you probably struggle with some of these same things as well as the many other examples I didn't mention.

— I know when I am partaking of (or initiating) things that aren't God's best, but it sure is easy to let it slide. I say I want to be holy, blameless, and beyond reproach, but often my actions disagree. We see gossip as social and rebellion as "edgy." We ignore the convictions that rise up throughout our days because we don't want to be the one to break up the party. Today—now, in fact, I want you to pray that God will reveal an area in your life where you have let sin slide. It might be in your marriage, your thought life, or even in the way you carry yourself in your Bible study group. Maybe it's an attitude of pride, a looseness in your speech, or a blatant sin act that you are keeping a secret. Pray that the Lord will be very specific in pointing out the places where you need to remove sin. It's hard to be the one who starts digging around in the garden, but I assure you the harvest is worth the effort.

Even if you don't feel comfortable going into specifics, it's important to share this with someone else who can help to hold you to a higher standard. When you start pulling up those weeds, you can be sure Satan has more waiting underneath to tempt you. Don't give up. Keep attacking those areas and remembering the potential that lies on the other side. God is worthy of our efforts to make it beautiful here in the garden He has given us.

IMMEDIATELY

While walking by the Sea of Galilee, he saw two brothers,
Simon (who is called Peter) and Andrew his brother, casting a net
into the sea, for they were fishermen. And he said to them,
"Follow me, and I will make you fishers of men." Immediately they
left their nets and followed him.

—MATTHEW 4:18–20

He had just cast his net into the sea when he heard a voice.

"Follow me, and I will make you fishers of men."

He didn't know the voice, but something about it must have compelled him, because he dropped his net immediately and followed the stranger.

Of all people in Scripture, I think I relate the most to Peter. He loved deeply, intensely, and with tremendous devotion. But sometimes he said the wrong thing.

Okay, more than sometimes.

In any case, I think the word *immediately* used to describe Peter's reaction to Christ could be used to categorize quite a bit of what we see of Peter in Scripture. He's sort of clumsily "all-in" with his love. He was the first of the disciples to pipe up when Jesus asked the disciples if they knew who He was, and I imagine him responding a little like me as an eager middle-schooler, hand raised and ready to be praised for my answer. He was impetuous, but he meant well. Gold star, Peter.

I feel so emotionally charged when I read about Peter. There are so many details that stir me to tears because I feel like I'm there with him in it all.

In the water, net in hand.

I heard Jesus, and I dropped what I had been clinging to, even though it was all I knew at the time. I didn't spend a lot of time worrying about what I was going to do next, or where He was taking me. I'm either "all-in" or "not at all" myself.

Have you ever read the Bible and chuckled to yourself? I assure you, there is humor there if you allow yourself to imagine it. God is the author of humor, and I believe He snuck in a few good one-liners for all of us who appreciate wit and timing (hand raised; Gold star, Angie).

On the eve of His death, Jesus told the disciples He was going to wash their feet. It was clearly a sacred moment. As Jesus approached Peter, Peter resisted Him. He told Jesus that He would never wash his feet. We extremists like to be really clear. You know, immediately. I can imagine this statement was accompanied by head shaking or some other physical motion to emphasize that it was not going to happen. This was Jesus! The Son of God certainly didn't need to be washing anyone's feet. Peter saw that and spoke up. Never. Never. NEVER. As in, not ever. Not now, not in a million years. It wasn't happening.

Well, Jesus responded to him that unless Peter submitted to Jesus washing him, then he would not truly be with Jesus.

Peter replied to this realization with, "Lord, not my feet only but also my hands and my head!" (John 13:9).

Umm, okay. So maybe "never" was a little bit strong. And now that I've had a few seconds to reconsider, let's go ahead and do the whole shebang, huh? Why stop with the feet? If You want this to happen, I'll grab some shampoo and body wash, and we'll call it a day. Sweet Peter. He goes from "never" to "head-to-toe" faster than most people can tie their shoelaces.

I get it. I mean, I totally, completely get it.

One of my favorite stories in the entire Bible, and it involves Peter. If you want to read it, it happens in Matthew 14. The short version is that Jesus told Peter to walk on water, so he stepped out of the boat in faith. He did okay for a little bit. Step by step he got closer to the Lord. But then he realized the waves were huge, and he doubted. He started to drown.

Yep. Been there.

I'm going to skip some of my favorite details for the sake of brevity, but it doesn't take long for Peter to reach out to Jesus, asking Him to save him from the sea.

And I love this.

I LOVE THIS (I'm fairly certain Peter would have loved italics and bold, capital letters)

"Jesus immediately reached out his hand and took hold of him" (Matt. 14:31). Immediately. The word that is used is *eutheōs*, and we see it approximately thirty times in the New Testament. One of the other occasions when it is used is when we read about the way Peter responded when he first heard the voice of the Lord.

Remember? He immediately dropped his net to follow. No dillydallying. Jesus called out to him, and he responded right away. Jesus was doing the same as Peter's faith wavered amidst the storm and waves. I can imagine that as Jesus' arm dove into the deep, Peter might have remembered what it was like to be a fisherman in desperate need of a Savior.

I know I do.

Peter wasn't born with the name "Peter," but rather, "Simon." Jesus Himself named him Peter, meaning "the rock." Does it surprise you at all that Jesus chose a man like Peter to be a "rock" of the faith? After all, let's not forget the epic failure Peter had yet to experience as his faith was challenged in the middle of the sea. It would not be long after when he would find himself at a dinner with Jesus washing his feet. At that same dinner, Jesus told Peter that he would soon deny Jesus three times in one day. Peter argued passionately, saying he would rather die than deny Christ. Oh, Peter. Not just "I won't do that, Lord," but "I WOULD RATHER DIE!" Well, at least he's consistent.

I can't help but wince when I read those words, because as we know, all the passion in that moment didn't translate when Peter was on the spot a few hours later. He did, in fact, deny his Christ three times. And when he heard the rooster crow, he remembered the Lord's words. He wept bitterly as he considered his betrayal.

Three times he said he didn't know Jesus just hours after He had washed his feet. What must it have been like on that dark night, or the three dark days to come, as Peter considered that he had been too weak to defend his King? As the Lord was beaten, hung to die, and His lifeless body buried in a cave, was Peter weeping over his actions somewhere else in the night?

Have you ever felt a shame that told you you weren't worthy to be near God? Maybe you've even thought you aren't good enough to be near the cross? I hasten to guess that you have. The enemy of our souls wouldn't have it any other way, I'm afraid.

Regardless of where he was during Jesus' crucifixion and death, his denial of Christ was not the last we heard from Peter. In fact, he became a great evangelist, proclaiming the name of Christ to people everywhere, no doubt in boldness. But what about the time in between? Did this man ever wonder if he could truly be forgiven for his sin?

The risen Christ revealed Himself to Mary the Magdalene, who ran to tell the apostles. For the most part, they didn't believe her. But there was one who did. "But Peter rose and ran to the tomb; stooping and looking in, he saw the linen cloths by themselves; and he went home marveling at what had happened" (Luke 24:12).

I would imagine it was immediately, wouldn't you?

Maybe he had the same thought I have, many times over.

Christ is real.

And that means there is still a chance for me to dedicate the rest of my life to Him, no matter how many times I have failed Him in the past.

So today, no matter how many times you've denied Him in word or action. No matter how far from the cross you feel. Come to Him immediately. Bring your sin, your shame, your past failures and know that by trusting in Him, His perfection, His death and resurrection, you will marvel at what He can do.

mending

— Do you see a lot of yourself in Peter? Obviously I do. I think one of the most important things we can do when analyzing our actions is to consider the fact that the intentions of our hearts matter to God. Sometimes I get so caught up believing that I am a bumbling idiot that I think He can't possibly use me anymore. But Peter . . . he denied his Christ! Not once, but three times. He cowered when he should have stayed strong, and he betrayed one of his dearest friends. Lest I think I would never do something like that, I am slapped in the face with my own haughty attitude. The consolation we have in considering our failures comes from knowing that He sees our hearts. It doesn't make what we have done right, no question. But it also doesn't separate us from Him if we have trusted in Christ.*

— Where are the places where you feel like you have burned the last bridge? Where there isn't a shred of hope left in you? The Lord wants to redeem these dark places and He wants to bring you to a place of wholeness with Him. Will you trust Him today to evaluate you at your deepest level? It has been my experience that the more we feel forgiven, the more we want to honor the Forgiver out of a sense of awe and love. Spectacular life comes from laying down all the things you wish you had done differently and then asking the Lord to strengthen you for the next leg of your journey. God hadn't given up on Peter, and He hasn't given up on you.

*If you aren't sure of your relationship with the Lord or don't know where to start, this would be a great time to flip back to the Foundational Pieces section and read, "My Jesus."

All In

*Then Jesus told his disciples, "If anyone would come after me,
let him deny himself and take up his cross and follow me.
For whoever would save his life will lose it, but whoever loses
his life for my sake will find it.*

—Matthew 16:24–25

 While we're thinking about lessons from the life of Peter, let's consider another account of him in Scripture. Peter was fishing, but he wasn't having much luck. He hadn't caught anything and neither had a single one of his companions. As dawn broke on a new day, they heard a voice that they didn't seem to recognize right away.

"Children, do you have any fish?" (John 21:5).

They told the stranger they didn't have any fish, and He suggested that they cast their nets on the right side of the boat instead. After they obeyed, they could not even pull the nets onto the boat because of how heavy with fish they were. As soon as this happened, everything clicked for John and he shouted, "It is the Lord!" (v. 7).

When Peter heard this, he put on an outer garment and do you know what he did then?

". . . he . . . threw himself into the sea" (v. 7).

Wait.

Threw himself?

Into the sea that had almost killed him?

Oh be still my heart. I love the imagery.

While the other disciples took the boat, dragging their load of fish, Peter jumped headfirst to get to Jesus. To be honest, I can't imagine doing it any other way. How spectacular that moment must have been! Think about the way it came together to reveal the heart of God to all of us.

1. Peter was fishing, just as he had been when he met Jesus.
2. Jesus called to him, and he came immediately.
3. He threw himself into the water because he had first-hand experience with a God Who knew exactly how to pull him out, should he need help.

Isn't it the same for us? Once we have seen the power of Jesus, we are much more likely to jump. Forget the fish and the nets. Who needs a boat? He's here, and I'm going to get to Him now. The Greek word for *threw* that is used in John 21:7 means "to give over to one's care uncertain about the result." Immediately, although Jesus was on the shore that must have been at least some distance away, Peter gave himself over to the One who saved him. Not only from the sea, but also from his sin. Wow.

It makes me want to throw myself into the sea over and over again. Whatever it takes to get to the shore. Not because it's safe.

But because He is there.

So, is that it? Problem solved. Once we know that we can trust Jesus to be there, we can take the leap of faith no matter the circumstances. Well, yes, that should be the case, but let's be honest. It isn't always so, not for Peter and not for us. Because somewhere in the back of my mind, even though I know Jesus is there, I wonder about something else. What if He doesn't receive me when I get to Him?

Do you ever feel like you crossed an invisible line in the sea and can't get to the shore? That you have finally pushed so hard that He has just given up on you?

Well, let's go back to Peter and see what we can learn. As far as we know from Scripture, when Peter threw himself into the sea, it was the first time he had seen Jesus since denying Him. Peter had sinned, but when faced with the opportunity to return to Christ, he did not hesitate. He leapt.

I wonder if he was worried about what Christ would say to him?

The Bible says that when they got to the shore, there was a fire burning. Now we can't know this for sure, but I can't help but wonder who built the fire. The disciples were in the boat all night, so it couldn't have been them. Even though it's a guess, my gut says that it was Jesus, and I'll tell you why I think so.

The Lord asked Peter to go get the fish from the boat so they could cook them. Peter obeyed Jesus and got the fish. They ate their breakfast, and when they were finished, Jesus turned His attention to Peter.

"Simon, son of John, do you love me?" One. "Yes, Lord; you know that I love you."

"Simon, son of John, do you love me?" Two. "Yes, Lord; you know that I love you."

"Do you love me?" Three. "Lord, you know everything; you know that I love you" (see vv. 15–17).

Do you think you have sinned one time too many?

He says it isn't so. He still calls to you from the shore. He still invites you to Him. And when you come, He welcomes you at His table. But He doesn't stop there. It isn't just that He received Peter, His questions also reflected that He would allow Peter to serve Him.

Do you remember the way the water felt when you couldn't breathe and you were all arms reaching and breath gasping? And do you remember when I pulled you out?

He asks me over and over if I love Him. As my lips say yes, He calls me to be a fisher of men. To feed His sheep. To remember the night He restored me and called me His own, despite my sin and my regrets. It's almost too much to bear. Who, Lord? Who am I to receive your mercy?

Here is what I would love for you to consider alongside me today. Are you allowing your sin to keep you from the cross? Has Satan whispered to you and told you that you've gone one step too far and that you can't possibly be restored?

This isn't the way the Lord sees you.

His desire is for you to throw yourself into the water. Leave your nets as many times as He asks and run where He calls you. In that place, you will be healed. And when you have been, I daresay you will have a story that is begging to be told.

"Now when they saw the boldness of Peter and John, and perceived that they were uneducated, common men, they were astonished. And they recognized that they had been with Jesus" (Acts 4:13).

Be bold, sisters.

Jump.

Immediately.

One.

Two.

Three.

mending

— Do you ever feel like the risk of drowning is more appealing than just jumping to someone who can save you? I don't know if it's our misplaced pride, our wounded ego, or (I suspect) a combination of both. We often underestimate our need for rescue, and in the interim, we unnecessarily tread water trying to figure out a back-up plan. Why is it so easy to believe that we are better off trying to do it on our own? The heart of our Savior is to release us from our certain death. We cannot possibly do that on our own. Where have you been resisting Him? Avoiding Him? Trying to pretend He doesn't know? Surrender it all to Him today and take the leap. He has a warm fire and a mission for you if you will trust Him with your life—all of it. Peter was never meant to stay on the boat believing He had forsaken the Lord. The freedom was there for him to have. As it is for you. I would hate to see another day go by without you realizing that the Lord wants to forgive you, to reinstate you, to give you a plan for tomorrow. Will you jump?

TREE OF MYSTERY

I believe that I shall look upon the goodness of the LORD in the land
of the living! Wait for the LORD; be strong, and let your heart take
courage; wait for the LORD!

—PSALM 27:13–14

 Just before Easter I was driving the kids over to see my parents, and we were talking about all the beautiful trees we passed that seemed to have blossomed overnight. The whole neighborhood had been transformed with bursts of lavender, pink, and pure white. It looked like something out of a movie. A splash of petals blew across the road as we drove by, stirred loose by a cool gust of spring breeze, and we oohed and aahed at the Lord's handiwork.

"Which tree is your favorite, Kate?" I asked.

She pointed at a tall white tree that looked like it was covered with snowballs, keeping her finger pressed to the window as it faded out of sight. "That one is my favorite, Mommy."

Abby chose one that looked like hydrangeas. It might not have been. I know nothing of plants except that the mere sight of my face makes them wither and die. I'm pretty sure a rosebush

I planted a few years ago picked up its roots and replanted itself in our neighbor's yard—a woman known to wear a belt stuffed with gardening tools while she works, as well as a hat that's roughly the size of New Mexico. She even uses a little pad to kneel on.

I really can't blame the roses.

"How about you, Ellie? Got a favorite?" She watched as the houses passed by, and then a few seconds later I heard her say quietly, "That one, Mommy. That one's my favorite. It's the prettiest one on the whooooole street."

"Oh, I see it," I said. "Those pink leaves are such a cool color, aren't they? I would wear one of those behind my ear for a date with Daddy!"

"No, Mommy, not that one. The one next to it."

I slowed down the car because I hadn't really seen the one next to it. I asked her where she was looking.

"There. Right there."

I made a confused face and looked at her in the rearview mirror.

"I think it's dead, Mommy. It doesn't have anything on it. But it's the prettiest one."

I just sat and waited, fascinated by the fact that out of everything we were looking at—all the bursting, beautiful spring colors—this was the tree she'd chosen. "Tell me more, hon."

"Well . . . maybe it's just pretending to be dead. Maybe its flowers just haven't come out yet. It's kinda like it's keeping a secret. Nobody knows what it's going to do."

I sat stunned, with my hand on the gear shift, unable even to put it in drive because I so felt the presence of the Lord. He uses my girls so many times when He is speaking to me, and I know from experience it's best just to be still and soak it in. I smiled at her, instantly aware that she had said something I'd need to come back to ponder a bit more.

That night, as I settled in for some quiet time, I opened the Scripture to the Gospel of John—which, I must admit, is my favorite—and I began with the crucifixion, reading slowly, deliberately, ever mindful that the Lord was stirring in me a deeper understanding. I suppose I've read this account at least 45 million times (give or take 44 million or so). I know what happens next, and then next, and then next . . . okay, done. But as I moved this time into the part about Christ's resurrection, I started thinking about what Ellie had said. And I felt the story taking on new meaning for me.

Jesus died on a cross. He was prepared for burial and placed inside a tomb that was blocked by a stone. Early the next day, some of His followers went to visit the tomb, and He was gone. His linens were there, but He Himself was not. This is a very brief, very detail-lacking synopsis of the miracle of the resurrection.

But here's what I think is so very interesting . . .

We don't know exactly when He actually rose from the dead.

We don't know what happened in that dark tomb between Jesus and His Father. We haven't been given a visual for the exact moment of resurrection, other than the report that He arranged His linens neatly before He left—which I think is very polite of a man who just woke up from death. At some point in time, perhaps in the dark of night within that sealed tomb, a miracle happened. A secret. A beautiful truth His followers wouldn't be privy to until the next day.

Eventually, yes, they would realize the miracle. He would appear, and they would believe. He would ask for something to eat, Thomas would touch His wounds, and everyone would reach consensus that He had actually done what He said He'd do. But not before there had been a gap of time between the miracle itself and the moment when they were finally able to see the evidence of it.

A gap between death and new life.

And it struck me how, in a sense, we are living in that moment today. We are weeping in our homes, crying by an empty tomb, begging to see that we haven't been duped, that He isn't going to leave us to face the fact that it might have all been a hoax. We walk side-by-side with Him on the road to Emmaus, not knowing that He walks alongside us, unaware that the footsteps of the Holy are even now being imprinted next to ours.

We walk in that gap every day.

I think many of His followers were sure He was dead and gone, that they had been deceived. As far as I can tell, there weren't groups of people huddled around His tomb awaiting His exit. Instead, they were bundled up with their children, miles away, left with only their fears and doubts and imaginations while—guess what?

He was rising.

During those very moments.

The beautiful, resilient flower that we call our Christ was no longer dead, as He seemed.

I am shattered by the humble recognition that somewhere in the night, a divine plan is occurring I'm unaware of. While I tuck my children into bed and pray for Him to have His way with them, with me, and within my every thought, the witness of the resurrection tells me that miracles are being sown. Even now. Even in the dark.

And so I will remember the tomb. I will remember the long, winding roads I must walk to see His face. I will anticipate the moment when the bread is broken and I fall face-first before Him in worship.

I will continue to choose the tree that bears secrets.

I will not be enticed by the blooms that fade quickly, but will rather allow myself to live in the mind of a seven-year-old who realizes that the most amazing things we can see in this life are the parts that are hidden, waiting for rebirth.

I believe with all my heart that one day I will be in the presence of the One Who watches my Audrey, and I will thank Him for the moments He gave me here on this earth in the presence of a crooked, withered tree I could have given up on long ago.

And in that place, I will know the secret. I will understand the mystery. I will cling to its truth and bow my head in reverence.

Beautiful Savior, may all the world see You in the midst of the blooming and choose to believe that Your splendor is waiting, somewhere beyond the brittle branches. And may we live in such a way that we glorify the Man whose light once shone in the darkness of a tomb.

Soli Deo Gloria.

mending

— It makes me smile to imagine the Lord Himself taking a breath after He had been dead for days. I wish I could see it happen and take in the moment that happened so far from human eyes. While the world was hustling and moving, He was breathing in the forgiveness and restoration that God had promised. He did what He was sent to do and endured the separation that brought us union with His Father. Somewhere in the dark of night, there was a breath that welcomed Him back into this life. I think we can sometimes get so accustomed to hearing a story that we fail to really take in the reality of it. Given the complexity and mystery of all that happened in Christ's death and resurrection, that has to be true. These accounts in Scripture are meant to compel us to not only communicate the events as they occurred, but also to worship—to be swept off our feet in sheer adoration for the Father who rejoiced to breathe life into us. Do you see Him this way? Many years ago, Moses asked God to show him His glory, and I can't help but think that sometimes we miss the glory for lack of asking. I'm not talking about asking Him for signs or answers, but simply to leave us awestruck and on our knees in true recognition of His holiness. Lord, show us Your glory . . .

One Better

Above all, keep loving one another earnestly, since love covers a
multitude of sins. Show hospitality to one another without grumbling.

—1 Peter 4:8–9

 For the record, it was Todd's fault.

I don't even remember the specifics of our "disagreement," but I am quite confident he was in the wrong. I don't back down as readily as some of my "really good at being submissive" friends do, and I recognize that it's something I need to be better at doing. For some strange reason, I seem to forget this factoid when I am knee-deep in self-righteous bickering and convinced that I am one witty comment away from victory.

But this particular night, I bit my tongue. I stepped on my pride momentarily and offered the kind of olive branch that is (sadly) uncharacteristic of me when I am mad (and also when I'm right, just in case you hadn't picked up on that part). I saw Todd's face settle, assessing me in order to see if this was just a gimmick to lead up to my final blow, and it made me cringe. He knew that I could, and he was waiting because he assumed that I would.

But I didn't.

I told him I was sorry and that I didn't think it was his fault. (That part was kind of a lie. As previously stated, I was convinced he was in the wrong. Carry on.)

As I looked at his face softening, I thought about the day I walked down a long aisle to get to him, knowing he was the only one I would ever love this way. And what in the world was I thinking right now? That somehow me proving how smart I was would change our marriage and make him look at me the way he did from the other end of the church?

So I stopped myself. I took a breath and apologized.

And in my head I heard the words, *You can do one better.*

And I did. In fact, I did more than one better, because as soon as I started going, I couldn't stop. All I desired was to feel like I had built him up and swallowed my own ugly pride. It turned out well, as you can imagine, and I walked away from it feeling like I had done the right thing.

I'm not saying it's easy, but these two words have helped me make some really good and life-giving choices over the past several weeks:

One better.

I walked through the family room and noticed a cup on the floor. I absentmindedly picked it up and started to walk to the sink.

One better, Ang.

So I went back, straightened the pillows, quickly gathered the books scattered on the ground, and deposited the kids' shoes in the shoe bin where they belong.

My friend called to tell me about her business trip, and all I could think was that I had deadlines that were crushing me and I didn't have time for the details. I caught myself, closed the computer, and told her I wanted to go on the porch so I could focus on what she was saying.

That's *one better.*

My daughter came to me after having her feelings hurt, and I had a great talk with her. I mentioned Scripture I thought would help her, I hugged her, and I told her I wanted to pray for her. It was good, but I knew I could just do *one better*. So I asked her if she wanted to go get a hot chocolate at the coffee shop down the road. We had a blast. When we got home, Todd had started making dinner, and I told him I appreciated it.

And then I deliberately walked over to him, took his face in my hands, and told him what a good man he was.

It's hard to do everything, but it isn't hard to just do *one better*.

Make a note to yourself today and hang it where you will see it. As you walk through the day, instead of feeling like you can't do it all, just remember: you don't have to do it all.

You will not believe the way these two little words will start to shape your hours and your heart. So go ahead, do *one better*.

I dare you.

No wait, I DOUBLE dare you. (See? It works for everything!)

mending

— I bet you can figure out what I'm going to ask you to do today, can't you? *One better*. That's it. You don't have to change the world in one swoop, but little things add up fast. You will start to see a difference very quickly. At the end of your first day, send a quick note or call a friend to relay what you worked on today and how you saw a change. Come on! You can do it!

TEACUPS

You make known to me the path of life; in your presence there is fullness of joy; at your right hand are pleasures forevermore.

—PSALM 16:11

 At the time I am writing this we are a week away from going to Disney World. Todd will be singing as part of an Easter morning worship service, and things were able to work out for the entire family to go along. For our three big girls it will be their second trip to Disney World. The first time was when we went with our extended family while I was carrying Audrey. Recognizing that was likely our only time with Audrey, those months were precious. We lived life with her, experiencing things as a family and telling her all about life. The girls wanted to show her Cinderella's castle, so despite the difficulty of the time, we were able to work out a trip with our extended family.

While we were at Disney World, I just felt sad for a lot of the trip. The emotions of the impending loss were always there. Yet, it was also a trip with so many wonderful memories as well. The girls laughed and rode and ate and stared. They marveled at Cinderella's castle the way I did when I was a little girl. To our surprise, they rode a roller coaster (hands up) nine times in a row. They could not get enough of "It's A Small World," but quickly decided that the real-life princesses were a combination of creepy and "not really the real princesses." They danced in every wide-open space they came across and devoured enough sugar to keep a small country running. In short, they were as happy as I have ever seen them. And through the lens of their joy, God impressed upon me a perspective I want to share with you.

On the first full day we were there, the girls rode the teacups. My father-in-law and I decided to watch instead of riding. I had the best time seeing everyone loop around the line as they waited for their turn. I was immediately struck by the pattern that emerged. Just as I sat down, I saw a couple arguing over whether or not to ride. They decided to go for it, but not before she had leveled him verbally and their little boy was staring off into space. Shortly after, I saw a delicate little flower of a girl stomp on the ground because she wanted the lavender teacup, "NOT the pink!!!!!" Her mother patted her hair (gently, around the 7-foot bow) and promised they would ride again and again until they secured the coveted cup. Princess climbed in as another couple started up in the background.

They had special tags to ride at a certain time and were irritated that they were going to have to wait another turn. Junior was the type of child that I try to steer my children away from at the park. He had a look of fierce anger than belied his little body—like a live wire in a preschooler, fueled by the attention that he could summon instantaneously. It was obvious his parents were more worried about his response to the wait than the wait itself.

As I watched all of these minidramas (and others) unfold, the most beautiful, unusual thing continued to happen.

As soon as the ride started and the music filled the pavilion, people just forget why they were unhappy. There was a forty-five second time period every few minutes where they just got lost in the blur of joy. Hands up, screaming laughter, cameras flashing. Even Junior got in on the action.

I love the teacups.

For the better part of a minute, all of the world is just right. It doesn't matter that you waited half an hour, or that you pretty much paid $50 for one go-round. It is totally insignificant that your problems are on the other side of the music. Everything is just a whirly-twirly perfect place.

And then it happens. Every time. Go for yourself and watch, because if you let yourself, you will see and feel the moment when the cups slow down and the music surrenders, and there is a collective sigh that summarizes the moment. Nobody wants it to end, they just want to keep spinning and spinning, except that you can't. It has to end. You have to get back to life, to hurt, to silence. To whatever it was that made you run there in the first place.

In a sense, that was my experience of the whole park. I wanted to get away, to escape and go somewhere magical, to get caught up in the idea that everything was just right.

I realized about five minutes into the fireworks on that trip four years ago that I had gotten on a plane to travel to a place where Audrey was healthy. A place where the joy that comes in forty-five seconds of spinning teacups doesn't stop when the music does. But it doesn't work that way.

The happiest place on earth is not on this earth.

This life is never going to fill us, is never going to satisfy our need for goodness. And it doesn't need to.

He is enough.

I am not someone who has it all figured out. I will not pretend that I am. What I am is a woman who realizes more and more every day that I want Jesus more than I want the teacups to keep spinning. In this life, we are going to be disappointed. We will hurt. But there is great joy in the One who works through our hurts.

If you are hurting today, I pray that you allow the Great Physician to heal your brokenness as He has healed so much of ours. If you are enjoying the ride, hold on tight and soak in all you can for the moment when it stops.

We will head back to Disney World next week and be there on what would have been Audrey's fourth birthday. There's not a moment I don't want her here with us. There's also not a moment when I don't know that He's enough. He has brought so much joy in the midst of the pain. Joy that has lasted much longer than the teacups and is but a shadow of that to come.

Joy that defies this world and welcomes the next with the eagerness of a child. Eternal, unending joy. It's ours for the taking.

mending

— I remember being almost asleep in my grandmother's apartment in Florida when my parents came sneaking into the room. My sister and I shared a pull-out bed in the den, and we both sat up as soon as the door creaked. "Girls, guess what? We have a surprise . . . we're going to DISNEY WORLD tomorrow!!!!" Jennifer and I both screamed and hugged them. I think I cried. Any extreme emotion in me leads to crying. It's just what it is. I remember thinking my life could not get any better. I couldn't sleep and we kept giggling and wishing the sun would hurry up so we could pack up the old Taurus wagon and hit the road. The anticipation was as great as the experience in a lot of ways. I'm sad to say that as an adult, it's a lot harder to feel the same kind of pure joy as I did when I was little. I suspect that's true for all of us. By the time we hit adulthood, we just know too much about the reality of living in a sin scarred world to pretend well anymore. Our trip to Disney World while I was carrying Audrey was a great reminder that we are in the interim. The best really is yet to come. As you go about the coming day, try and remember that it is part of the "anticipation" phase of life. The best is going to be here before we know it—and it's going to be much better than anything that could keep us awake all night in this life.

THE REEDS

As we sat down for church, I noticed that the name of the sermon was "Providence." I felt my body start to settle as our pastor opened in prayer. I love to be in church, where His peace settles upon me in the most profound ways, each song tugging me closer to the feet of my sweet Lord. The message on this particular Sunday was about the birth of Moses.

You may know the story by heart, but I often find that God can bring new application from biblical stories I've heard a thousand times, so indulge me as I walk through the story and share something that struck me as my pastor preached on the birth of Moses. Try not to think about the man—the prophet, in fact, he grew to be—and instead just follow the story.

Moses was born to a Hebrew woman during the rule of a cruel Pharaoh who demanded that all Hebrew boys be put to death. Yet, Moses' mother was able to hide him with her for about three months after his birth. I can imagine that she must have feared for the time when he would be found in their Hebrew household and killed. When she could not hide him any longer, she put him in a papyrus basket and placed it among the reeds in the Nile River.

Moses' sister watched from a distance so she would know what happened to the baby as he sat in the basket nestled in the reeds by the riverbank. At the same time, Pharaoh's daughter was bathing in the Nile, and she saw the basket in the reeds and asked one of her handmaidens to bring it to her. So here we have the daughter of the man who has ordered all Hebrew baby boys be killed, and she happens upon a baby who fits that exact category of condemned. She was a girl from wealth, power, and privilege. She surely knew the expectation that she would uphold all that her father had declared. Even if that meant murdering a baby.

So what did Pharaoh's daughter do when she saw three-month-old Moses? Call for her father's soldiers to kill the baby?

She opened the basket and discovered the baby, who was crying. Scripture says that she recognized he was a Hebrew child, but rather than order his death, she took pity on him. At that moment, Moses' sister stepped out from where she had been watching and asked Pharaoh's daughter if she should go find a Hebrew woman to nurse the baby. Pharaoh's daughter agreed, and off Moses' sister went to get her mother to come and serve as the nurse for the baby—her own son. Pharaoh's daughter, not knowing that the baby's new nurse was actually his mother, even paid her for the service. After she weaned the boy, he was brought back to Pharaoh's daughter, who raised him as her son. She named him Moses, which means "drawn out of the water."

That is the story of how a baby boy, a Hebrew who should have been killed at birth, becomes Egyptian royalty. It has been said, "She put him in the river a slave, and he was brought out of the water a prince." I can imagine that as his mother set the basket in the water, tears streamed down her face and she wondered if she would ever see him again. Out of her hands, into the water. What an incredible act of trust in a sovereign God.

Moses, as you may know, grew up to be God's prophet to His people—a man to whom God gave much of His law and spoke face to face, as someone speaks to a friend. Given such an extraordinary relationship with the Creator of the universe and the circumstances of Moses' birth, he must have had a sense of the extraordinary means God had used so often in his life. It was from this perspective of trust in the Mighty One that Moses often led the Israelites.

One of the most amazing examples of this leadership is in Exodus 14 when the Israelites were fleeing from Egypt only to look back and see Pharaoh's army approaching. The sea was ahead of them, the army behind, and all of a sudden the slavery they were fleeing seemed appealing. The fear was overwhelming, the circumstances impossible, and the outcome seemed certain. They begin to complain to Moses and point out that the circumstances were overwhelming. Exodus 14:14 captures Moses' response: "The LORD will fight for you; and you only have to be silent."

Many, many times I have recalled this verse and rested in knowing that my God, my Strong Tower, is in battle for me. I need only to be still.

A baby was drawn out of the water to be used by our Lord. God had great things planned for him. The providence of the Lord allowed his mother to keep him hidden at his birth, ordained that Pharaoh's daughter would be bathing at the exact time his basket would be in the reeds to draw her attention, and made sure Moses' sister was near enough to connect them all back to Moses' mother. It is beautiful to see them in my mind's eye, as the Lord orchestrated the life of Moses.

From the life of Moses we can see the sovereignty of God, who uses the details of life to bring about His plans. For Moses this meant being rescued as a baby and used mightily for the Lord. And oftentimes for us His providence leads to experiences on this earth that bring great joy and deliverance as literal as what the Egyptians experienced when God fought for them and parted the sea. Is that it? Promise of happiness for all?

Well, not so quick. Moses led God's people through the wilderness, but he never got to experience the Promised Land himself. Just as for Moses, our lives are also a mixture of circumstances that lead us to rest and revel in the providence of God, and circumstances that drive us to our knees and question how such things could happen. Never have I known this so profoundly as I did during the time that I sat in church and heard the sermon on the birth of Moses three months after the loss of our daughter.

My mind was screaming these words . . .

Where, oh great providence of God, were you when my daughter's kidneys began to fail?

I was there, in the river, basket in hand. Where were you, Lord?

I could feel the anger rising up in me as I listened, wondering why the God of the reeds, the God of papyrus, the God of Moses chose something different for my family. I was still, and yet He chose not to overcome the battle we were facing. My heart was bursting from within me, and the tears were hot on my cheeks.

I believe with everything in me that He could have changed our story and saved Audrey as miraculously as He did Moses. This line of thinking inevitably brings me to the question, Why didn't He?

I have absolutely no idea.

What I do know is this.

The Lord walks beside me as He walked beside Moses. He knows me by name. He loves me and I love Him. I pushed my baby through the reeds and never saw her again. And yet, here I am, worshipping the God who allowed it. I still believe that He will fight for me and that I can be still. I believe in the providence of God, even when it feels contrary to what my heart desires.

I have seen the way my Audrey has brought people to the cross. I have seen the way she has impacted my own life, and the lives of people I may never meet. It doesn't mean I don't want her back, or that I never hurt or doubt. I do. You may not have lost a child or been faced with slavery as the Israelites have, but I'm certain you have faced circumstances that felt overwhelming. You have lived with things you wish you could have changed. And you have probably questioned why God would allow you to experience such things.

Scripture says that the Lord Himself buried Moses, and to this day, nobody knows exactly where his body lies. We do not know what Moses said to God as he breathed his last breath, but we know that he fulfilled his purpose on this earth.

In his case, it was 120 years. In Audrey's, it was less.

None of us knows how long we have or how many trials we will face. We do not know whether we will see victory on this earth or in eternity. You can know the God who knows all of this, though. The God whose hand was on Moses' in the basket has His hand on you. Be still and let Him fight for you. Trust not in your circumstances, but in His power to overcome.

He has not abandoned you, and He has not abandoned me. He is the God powerful over the universe. He is the God powerful over broken dreams and hopeless situations. He created you.

Be still and let Him fight for you.

mending

— I am not sure why, but I tear up whenever I think of God burying Moses. Their relationship was so intimate, and I long to have that kind of peace. To have a relationship so sacred that in my very last moments here, as I whisper good-byes to the only world I've known, that I would only see Him. This life to the next. Are you scared of death? I have to admit that at times I am. Yet, in one way or another, we all get to have the experience that Moses did. We will feel peace, receive comfort, and welcome His arms around us as we move from this world to the one with Him. Is this an area where you struggle? Seek refuge in His Word today by reading the following passages: Psalm 46:1-2, Psalm 48:14, Psalm 73:26, John 6:39–40, Romans 8:31–39, 1 Corinthians 15:50–57, and Isaiah 40:28–31.

— Welcome the peace that comes from laying down our struggles and trusting Him with the unknown details. He is not unknown. Nothing about this life is happenstance, our deaths included. God wasn't surprised when Audrey took her last breath, and I believe she was ushered into the presence of God in perfect peace. I have to still myself and listen to His promises in order to combat the fears I have . . . let me encourage you to do the same, not by your own strength, but through the power of the promises in His Word.

Sketched

*He has made everything beautiful in its time. Also, he has put
eternity into man's heart, yet so that he cannot find out what God
has done from the beginning to the end.*

—Ecclesiastes 3:11

 One of my favorite games growing up was play-
ing mommy with my dolls. I would take them
everywhere. I remember my favorite doll, Abby,
and how I would even take her along in the car.
It was perfect. I would buckle her in, smile, and
dream about the day when she would be a real daughter.

Later I would pull out all the dishes I could get my hands on,
set up place settings for my five or six favorite dolls, and invite
them all to kindly come to dinner. I would change their outfits
because I felt like dinner should be more fancy than their playtime
outfits. I would giggle and move them in and out of their seats,
help them pick up empty milk cartons, and excuse them when they
had finished their supper.

I was sketching what it would be like when those dolls came
to life and came to my real house, with my real husband. I would
giggle, set them in their beds, and dance beside them—all the

while wondering what they would be like when they were five, ten, or eighteen. What their first dates would be, and how they would break our hearts, because little girls always do, you know.

I won't say I was a dreamer, for truly I never have been. Dreaming sounds far away and impossible, so I think I prefer to think of it as sketching. I have the gist of a situation, the outline and form. I don't know the details because I haven't seen them yet, but there is room for hope in all the lines. There isn't color because I'm not in charge of how things will be. I'm just a girl who has lived her life with a nicely sharpened pencil. And while this girl goes through today, she is always (always) sketching tomorrow. Dreamers dream big, and I love that. But I don't. Really. And it's okay. I just want to have an outline and an eraser and a few things to inspire me enough to pull the covers off of me on a cold winter morning.

It isn't always easy to be a sketcher. It's art and it's beautiful. It's all heart and love and wishing. The problem is that sometimes you get to the frame you've imagined as one way or another and you weren't right at all. No matter how you try to erase and redraw, you can't change it to what you imagined.

Do you sketch?

Before we had children, we found this lovely farm near our house, and we fell in love with it. I imagined taking my kids there for giant pumpkins and running around while laughing and breathing in fall. We had the twins, and I couldn't wait for our celebration at the farm. It wasn't long and the time had come to go as a family. There were games to play, sun to soak in, and the joy of another long-awaited autumn breeze. It was just as I had always sketched.

The twins were in bright orange outfits with pigtails. Nobody could tell them apart, and we even mixed them up in some of the photos. They were holding pumpkins, loving the smell of cider, and we were Mommy and Daddy.

Just Mommy and Daddy.

Another year passed, and then another. A new baby came along, which changed the sketch. But there had always been room for her. We just didn't know how to draw her eyes and her lips, or her sweet, deep, full laugh. And then, there she was. We went back to the farm the following year, and yes, one more pumpkin please. We smiled, set them on a wagon, and waited for three sweet smiles. We got them, despite Ellie being sick. I still love that photo, because she was trying so hard to look happy and she just wasn't.

Years drift and the farm stays the same. Then I was pregnant again, sketching life, and then the Lord told us that particular drawing would be altered. We know He loves us, but it's sad. It's sad because I wanted to bring my new baby to the farm that we go to every fall. That's what I'd sketched.

Time slipped away after we lost Audrey, and we got lost for a while. But we knew there was the farm and all of the right, normal things that make for photo albums and childhood memories, so we went back. Every year we went back. Because they love Jesus at this little (actually, not-so-little) farm, and they love the company that floods it in the fall. It is such a happy place.

This past fall was sketched for me before I had the chance to pick up a pencil. As the days passed, I became sad. I realized that for the first time I wasn't going to get to take the girls to Gentry's Farm. I was so sad because it was something that always had been, and you know how beautiful those "always things" are, don't you?

I didn't get to go this year, and I was so broken over it. Not for missing the farm, but for the mommy who had always had a sketch of family being together. That's what makes it so special, but I was working. Did I fail them? Did I, girls? I asked them, and they shook their heads no. I remember them doing so because I made a new sketch called grace, where I knew they knew my love. And I let that sketch be just as it was. Which is always the way grace should be.

Our sketch for Gentry's Farm wasn't the only one that was disturbed this past year. When Todd's tour schedule was adjusted, the twins' birthday fell right in the middle of a leg when he couldn't get home and we couldn't get to him. We were supposed to all be together. That's how we sketched it, but not how it worked out. Mommy was there, but Daddy was not. Sometimes I feel like I can't see straight because everywhere I look there are more mistakes on the drawings. Have we failed?

And then the birthday came, and we celebrated nine years of life with good friends and, of all things, painting. We talked about what they wanted to paint and why they chose those colors and shapes. I saw in them the same thing I see in myself. This is what I want it to look like . . .

But I know that it might not turn out that way. I want them to know that the beauty is in the work and the love—not perfect lines.

I want the girls to know that they are loved and that we would always choose them. But I also want them to consider the beauty of what God does with the sketch when we hand over the pencils.

As we gathered our things to leave the painting adventure on their birthday, I was wistful. I had been watching their eyes as they painted, and they were so intent. They were so convinced and pur-poseful. I had used the opportunity to talk with them about what it means to imagine a picture and see God complete it in His way. They ran out of the shop and were speaking to a sweet man when I follow them out. I heard one of them say, "It's us!" I leaned over and saw the most exquisite sketch.

He had been there for a few minutes and saw my sweet chil-dren with their friends and decided to draw them to give to me. He had a twinkle in his eye, and the kids thought he was great. I didn't know why, but I wanted to cry. All I managed to get out was to tell him that their father is a musician who was on the road, missing their birthday for the first time. I told him we have both missed things this year, which has been so hard. We talked for a bit, and he handed me the drawing when it was done. It was an incredible drawing, and then I saw his name, very small, on the bottom of the image. It was a last name, so I ask what his first name is.

"Jimmy," he said with a smile.

I looked back down, and then I saw the letters come into focus. *Gentry.*

He spoke, explaining that I might have heard of his farm. I forgot that I can't really see God with my own eyes because I knew in that moment that He had chosen to speak to me. I was weak with love, knock-kneed and speechless that I was being wooed by the King. Mr. Gentry didn't even know that Jesus was speaking through his pencil and his twinkling eyes, but I did. I do.

"Yes sir, I do know your farm. And this is the first year I haven't been able to come with my children. We love it there."

He smiled. It is a very popular place in this area, with thousands of visitors. I couldn't put all of it into words before I got to my car, but when I did, I got choked up and I stilled myself. Stilled the thoughts that had been haunting me about my mothering and all of my sketches being distorted. I just listened. He spoke. I didn't hear Him, I just felt the words enter my mind and heart, and I knew them to be true.

When you are doing what I've asked you to do, you don't have to worry about getting to the farm. I'll bring you the farmer instead. And when you think you have lost sight of all your sketches, just know that it's okay. I know where the sketches are, what they need to be, and I will never leave you.

Let go of the grief and the sorrow. Release the anger and the plans set in stone. Because I hold your sketch in My hand the way Mr. Gentry did in his. I watch and I draw—even when you don't know. I am concerned with all things that concern you.

My tight grip has loosened and I have surrendered this season to Him. He has shown me in such a magnificent way that I don't want to sketch the way I used to. Consider with me what it would mean for the sketches we cling to if we recognized that God is not only watching over us, but also holding the sketch Himself. The sketches from an all-knowing, all-consuming, all-loving and mighty God must be spectacular.

So join me in letting go of the pencil and putting away the sketch pad.

Not planning, not drawing. Just sitting and enjoying the hand of my Father.

He makes all things beautiful.

mending

⁓ The heart of this experience, and so many others that He has given me, is that He is the Artist and we are the feeble pencil in His hand. I need not worry myself sick about the way it looks, because He is in control of it. It's such a simple sentence, and has the tendency to sound trite. But the all-consuming beauty of the picture He is creating leaves me breathless. I don't have to scribble and scratch my way through life feeling like it's up to me to make all the ends meet. My job is to walk in obedience, always seeking His will. Simple. Well, simple to say, at least! What is a situation that you are facing right now that feels out of control? Where you are tempted to believe that your responsibility is to fix things? Is it possible that what the Lord is asking you to do is really to allow Him some room to mend some things that are broken? Rest in His Word today. He is in the business of making all things new and working all things together for the good of those who love Him.

— The Bible teaches that it is the sword of the Spirit with which we can defeat all that threatens our walk with the Lord. Bring this reality home as you memorize 2 Corinthians 5:17 and Romans 8:28.

HE LOVES YOU

For I am sure that neither death nor life, nor angels nor rulers,
nor things present nor things to come, nor powers, nor height nor
depth, nor anything else in all creation, will be able to separate us
from the love of God in Christ Jesus our Lord.

—ROMANS 8:38–39

I have always loved the verse that says God cares about us more than sparrows (see Matt. 10:29–31). I'm not sure I've always believed it, though.

For the longest time I kept it to myself, always nodding at the right time while in Christian circles, furrowing my brow in agreement when it was brought up. As if I was considering the depths of this unfathomable love, and swallowing it like sweet tea in the hot sun.

Delicious.

But that wasn't what I was thinking.

I was actually imagining what it must be like to honestly believe God would love me that way.

Those girls in Bible study had their act together. And all I had was a Bible that had brand-new stuck-together pages and a date with a guy who couldn't remember my last name.

I decided it was a complicated last name and stifled the desire to be known by either one.

But the image of a sparrow chased me everywhere I went.

Years passed.

Decades, in fact.

I continued to believed that a God Who would love someone like me wasn't worth loving back. And one day, over a cup of too-cold coffee, I decided I wanted to know what it was that made this bird so important. I had gone through a very dark time in my life, and I was looking for Him, for answers, for a reason to believe He even cared, let alone loved me.

Quite frankly, I wasn't that worried about love.

I just wanted to know I existed to Him.

Why would He care about the number of tears I cry, or the hairs on my head? I just wanted Him to know I cried at all.

I waited on Him.

After about an hour, I came across an article on a particular type of bird. It wasn't a Christian reference, but rather a zoological-type resource with statistics and pictures for someone who knows much more about birds than I do.

I skimmed it until I came across a sentence that explained how this certain type of bird learned how to sing. I didn't finish reading it before the tenderness overcame me.

And this particular bird cannot learn to sing in the daylight because it is always concerned with the chatter around it. Instead, its cage must be covered so that it is in complete darkness. Then, it is able to hear its master and will learn to sing.[5]

More than a sparrow.

More than the pitch-black darkness.

He loves me.

And in that place of feeling left alone, unwanted, disregarded, abandoned, He whispered to my weary soul.

Sing, love.

In the black night, I listened to His voice and I heard Him in a way I never had before. I stopped trying to focus on the silhouettes around me, panicked and desperate for my bearings. I accepted the fact that it might be a long while before I knew where I was and how to find my way back. Slowly, I started to believe that He treasured me enough to trust my voice in the dark. Nobody watching, nobody to judge.

Just me and the One Who told me I was worth it.

Have you heard Him too? I pray so.

Sing, love.

Despicable as the shadows may be, they hold the promise of the Master's voice. Worry not about tomorrow, wondering if the sun will come again.

It will, as it always does, in some sense or another.

In the meantime, raise your voice to the One Who loves you.

He loves you.

It isn't too late to fill the sky with the sound of song. And when you do, know I will be not-so-far away, joining in with you as we await the dawn.

Sing, love.

The Master is listening.

mending

— What choice can you make to "sing in the dark" today? Is there a particular situation you are facing that is troubling you, but that you've struggled to believe would merit the care of God? It's easy to see ourselves as insignificant when we look around, but the truth is, He hears you. Every broken prayer that comes from heartache, every single tear that falls from disappointment. He desires for you to be conformed to His image and will use all of the tiny details, struggles, and victories to bring about that purpose. Let your prayer be this: "Lord, I believe that you see me when I am in the shadows, doubled over with grief and the temptation. I am choosing to believe what you say instead of my emotions. I will not allow the enemy to convince me otherwise. Fill me with your peace and reassurance. Amen."

— Do you have a friend who really seems to struggle with feeling worthy of God's love? Pray that the Lord would speak to that person and remind them that she isn't forgotten or unusable. Ask Him to reveal any areas of her life that are standing in the way of accepting this love, and pray that she is able to begin tearing down the walls and allowing His grace to flood her to overflowing. Follow up with a phone call, e-mail, or text, and just let her know that you are thinking of them. If a Scripture comes to mind, be sure and pass that along as well.

THE TYRANNY OF CHOICE

*Indeed, I count everything as loss because of the surpassing worth of
knowing Christ Jesus my Lord. For his sake I have suffered the loss of
all things and count them as rubbish, in order that I may gain Christ
and be found in him, not having a righteousness of my own that
comes from the law, but that which comes through faith in Christ,
the righteousness from God that depends on faith.*

—PHILIPPIANS 3:8–9

It was a week before Christmas, and I was frozen in the Barbie aisle with no relief in sight.

Did she say she wanted the one with the red dress or the blue dress?

A perky woman passed by, and without a care in the world, she reached for the winter-dress Barbie, double-checked her list, and threw the doll in her cart. Sigh. Why didn't I write it down when she said it?

I agonized for another few minutes, holding the blue in one hand and the red in the other.

Red. Blue. Red. Blue.

Nothing.

Merry Christmas.

The day after Todd and I came back from our honeymoon, we made our inaugural trip to the grocery store as a married couple. I would love to say we reached for the same loaf of bread and giggled at the way we were made for each other.

There was a sweet moment as I was walking through the hair section, trying to choose a shampoo and conditioner. I popped open a bottle and sniffed it. Todd smiled. "I'm going to run and get some yogurt. I'll be right back," he said. I closed the cap and reached for the next bottle. "Okay." I kissed him on the cheek and smiled back. I don't know why I smiled. Nothing was really cute about the situation, but looking back, it may have been the fact that my newlywed self weighed about as much as your average fourth grader. That's a reason to smile all in itself.

He walked out of sight, and I continued my quest. A few minutes later I saw him at the end of the aisle, grinning from ear to ear at his precious bride.

"You ready?" he called down.

"Almost. Let me just look for a few more minutes." I waved, and he disappeared again. Adorable.

This continued for about six more passes.

"Ang?"

This time he looked afraid. And I'm not saying there is anything wrong with that.

"Hmm? What? Hey, does this have a good vanilla smell or a bad vanilla smell?" I replied, oblivious to the look of man-panic that had overtaken him.

He hovered over the bottle and avoided eye contact, considering the fact that not only did he need to come up with the correct answer about $4 shampoo smells, but also that he was looking at another fifty-plus years of wandering around the store while crazy-pants sniffed for three hours. It was, to say the least, a rude awakening.

Simply stated, we are inundated with the tyranny of choice.

How can a trip to the store turn out okay when you are faced with fifty-seven grape jelly options? In what world is that necessary?

What if you get the reduced-sugar grape jelly and it tastes horrible?

What if you married the wrong man?

I know this sounds like a drastic jump in situations, but I don't think it is. I've been convicted and overwhelmed over the nature of my humanity and the fickleness that is bred by entitlement.

It started a long, long time ago in a garden where God gave them what was good, but they didn't think it was good enough for them. The first man and woman felt entitled to choose what they wanted even when He had told them that choice was forbidden. They didn't need it. They weren't entitled to everything. He had given them everything they needed.

He had given them Himself.

I admit that standing in the middle of Target clutching two Barbie dolls and screaming "I only need Jesus!" might not be the best response to feeling overwhelmed by choice.

The ugly truth is that the color of that stupid dress mattered to Kate. At least I thought it did. In truth, she probably didn't remember. The whole situation made me ask myself if I was fostering a sense of entitlement in my children, not necessarily by giving them too much, but too many choices.

I have a degree in developmental psychology, and I've read almost every parenting book that exists on planet Earth. I know that choices are important to help our children form opinions and feel autonomy. Kate is not the easiest of my children. She is passionate and strong willed to the degree that water is damp. I'm the first to admit it and the last one to fall asleep because I am simply worn out. She can be a walking litmus test for patience. And I fail regularly.

She has inherited more than my dark brown eyes. She is paralyzed by the choices of the world, and one stop at the dollar spot will put her in a tailspin. We see the surface where it looks like an issue with "stuff," but there's more to it than that.

It is the drive inside us that longs for the tree we weren't supposed to have.

Not just in marriage, but in our jobs, our schedules, our finances, our homes, our cars, and our parenting style.

We are tempted to believe that we are one step away from the thing that makes everything else go away. If we can smell every single bottle of cheap shampoo we can get our hands on, we might find the one that makes him love us more. If we buy the right Barbie, then she won't remember the times I've not been patient.

When you expect a choice in every situation, you need to pause and consider what is driving you. Has God given you what you need? Are you being overwhelmed by a drive to choose from a tree He has forbidden?

I don't remember which Barbie she wanted.

I also don't remember the reason I thought it mattered all that much.

I don't need a thousand choices in this life. I need Him.

I'm desperate for Him, actually.

Adam and Eve were given the Garden of Eden. It had everything they needed. Yet, they chose that which separated them from God. At the risk of everything I write boiling down to the same thing, it always comes down to choosing Him. In a world overrun with choices, He is our choice. Give in to grief or trust Him? Doubt or obey? Escape into the choices or cling to only God? When you are tempted to feel overwhelmed by first-world problems and choices, whisper that word under your breath until you feel your bones ache with Truth. Him. Him. *Him*.

He gave Himself.

There's no time to wonder about what else He could have given you. Every bit of it is irrelevant in light of Him.

Live a life that loves Him back.

Choose well.

He is enough.

mending

— Do you get tangled up in your choices too? Do you feel like you have too many options and not enough willpower to make the right decision? Are you allowing the variety of choices to entice you to indulge in options that are not honoring to the Lord? Have you allowed your priorities to be overwhelmed by choices that seem innocent, but communicate a pattern of materialism or pride rather than reliance on the Lord? This is easy to do, but it can lead to distance between us and the Lord as we lean further into sin and away from Him. Perhaps as you read, something came to your mind as an area where you know you are being tempted to look toward an option the Lord has told you is off limits. Or maybe you are realizing more and more that controlling your choices is the one choice you will not give over to the Lord. Whatever it is that is keeping you from choosing Him and Him alone is the very thing that you need to guard against most. Spend some time focusing on the Lord, imagining yourself physically laying the options in front of Him and giving Him control over them. Ask Him to help you make the decision that most glorifies Him, and then follow through in obedience. And after that? Leave it alone and remember that no matter what, He is enough.

Ransomed

But when Christ had offered for all time a single sacrifice for sins,
he sat down at the right hand of God, waiting from that time until
his enemies should be made a footstool for his feet. For by a single
offering he has perfected for all time those who are being sanctified.

—Hebrews 10:12–14

 We all have things that we deeply regret, that we struggle with, that we wish we could do over. Yet, the amazing, life-defining truth is that the God I serve does not see me this way. He sees me as pure and clean, ransomed through the blood of Christ.

Ransomed. What a beautiful word.

Have you ever gone through a season in which you sense God is nudging you to a deeper level of commitment and trust? Could it be that this book is a part of Him doing just that? Part of moving forward is always letting go of what has held us back, and it is never less than a battle. There are days in life when we are forced to come face to face with what it is that binds us, and for me, that is fear.

I really struggle with fear.

It ebbs and it flows, and sometimes it seems to have disappeared, only to show up when I least expect it. In the months following Audrey's death, my anxiety was high, and I was also worried about my other children. I watched my kids closely, trying to anticipate their reactions to their baby sister's death. I was worried about the anxiety that may come to be a part of their lives as well. I would pray over them at night, and I watched their movements, their drawings, their responses to strangers, their sleeping patterns, their eating habits—everything.

I wanted to know how they were processing the loss, and I noticed several things that I was worried about. Kate seemed to be acting up more. Abby was making moral decisions that were more rebellious than usual. She always wants to test the boundaries. Ellie, on the other hand, was a whole different story. Ellie is my mother hen. She has tended toward worrying since she could see the world around her.

When Ellie was younger she would cry when she went to Sunday school because she didn't want to be away from us. She wants to know where the war is before she goes to bed. If Kate hits her, she lies and says it didn't happen because she doesn't want Kate to be punished. She asks if everybody is wearing their seat belts when we get in the car. I once walked out on the porch and saw her on our porch swing in a car seat. You know, because porch swings can be dangerous.

We went to Destin the summer after we lost Audrey and visited this neat little shopping place that had a bunch of fun stuff for kids. At that time especially, our kids didn't really like to do the whole "ride" thing. They have to be coerced to do anything that requires being a few steps away from Mommy and Daddy, and whatever it is most certainly must stay attached to the ground. Even Kate is not really up for adventure if it involves uncertainty. So when we passed by this huge apparatus that was charging thirteen dollars for a giant trampoline ride, I knew we had nothing to worry about.

Todd, on the other hand, decided that they might want to try it. It was absurdly expensive, but I knew that they would never go for it, so I smiled sweetly and told him it sounded like fun.

Kate? Maybe.

Abby? Seriously doubted it.

Ellie? I pictured my fear-of-flying self as a flight attendant and decided that was a likelier scenario.

Let me describe the "ride" a little further. It involved a harness and a man who acted as a rocket launcher while sending screaming children a little past Jupiter. My girls waited in the line, and I watched as they got closer and closer. Abby was first. She started to get a worried look on her face and looked at me.

"It'll be so fun!" I yelled. It didn't look like fun to me, but I didn't want Abby to be scared, so I smiled and gave her a thumbs up. She started jumping, and I saw her little face way up in the sky. Ellie watched with a look of horror, and then her face crumpled up. "I'm scared." She looked at me. She was trying to read my face.

I didn't want to say the first thing that came to mind because it felt weird to say, "Well, thank goodness, because that thing looks like a torture chamber and I would rather gnaw off my own arm before I let him launch me into the air." The whole arm thing seemed dramatic given the situation, so I opted for response "B."

"I think it might be fun if you try it, El. It's not supposed to be scary; it's supposed to be fun!"

You know how God whispers to you about three seconds after you give someone great advice that you yourself have been completely failing to follow? Well, it happened to me right then. What is she afraid of? I thought. That God will forget her in midair? That we will all pack up and leave while she jumps? That she will fall?

Wait, what am I afraid of? That God will forget me? That I will fall?

I once had the pleasure of sharing a meal with an amazing woman named Gracia Burnham. If her name sounds familiar, it is because she was the missionary from the United States who was taken hostage for a year in the Philippine jungle and who watched her husband die in the gunfight that saved her life. They had waited for over a year, trudging along with their captors, praying for their children back in the U.S., begging for mercy. They went through unspeakable hurt for months, waiting for someone to pay for them to be released. They were dirty, mistreated, hurt, and humiliated. They were waiting to be ransomed.

If you talk to Gracia about her experience, you will not sense fear, nor will you sense hostility. You will feel an indescribable feeling of forgiveness and peace, and above all, the kind of freedom that defies fear. The kind of freedom that knows that ransom is not paid with money.

It was paid with blood.

If you believe in Jesus, you can know what it feels like to trust completely in the One Who holds you high above the discernible ground. You know that life isn't always perfect, and it isn't always easy. It is entirely possible that something will give way, and you will fall headfirst into the ache that is this life.

But on the other hand, you'll never know unless you jump.

And that brings me back to my sweet Ellie. She did cry a little while watching her sister on the ride, but she was determined to give it a try. They put the buckles on her and she almost reconsidered. She looked like she was about to back out of it, but before I could scream "Refund!" I saw a look of determination come across her face. It is probably not too dissimilar to the expression that came across my face, years ago, as I told Jesus that I would believe.

What happened next I cannot describe with words, but I can tell you that I have seen the image of my joy-filled Ellie many times since that fearfully anticipated ride. It will forever be engraved in my mind as the moment when God whispered, *You have no idea what you would miss if you let this pass you by.*

Thank you, Jesus. We are no longer captives.

mending

— Without question, this is one of my favorite "kid stories" to date. It's amazing how God can use something so simple to bring truth. The hard part is really paying attention to life as it happens around you—whether it's your kids, your friends, your husband, or just people-watching at the coffee shop. He has given me so many gifts when I have simply been attentive to my environment and responsive to what He has put in front of me each day. It's not uncommon to hear the term "divine appointment" used, but I think we have underestimated what it really represents. Our lives are one divine appointment after another, and it's more a matter of how many we are being obedient in acknowledging. The question is not whether or not He is working around you. He is. The issue is whether or not you are listening with the expectation to hear Him. Make a point to listen starting now, inviting Him to teach you in even the most mundane tasks . . . an incredible relationship with the One True God is possible for all those who hear and follow His voice.

— Saturating ourselves in God's Word is one of the most amazing tools He gives us in our walk with Him. John 10:27 is an incredible reminder as we seek to train ourselves to be responsive to how the Lord is speaking to us. "My sheep hear my voice, and I know them, and they know me" (John 10:27).

THE THRESHING FLOOR

He restores my soul.
He leads me in paths of righteousness
for his name's sake.
Even though I walk through the valley of the shadow of death,
I will fear no evil,
for you are with me;
your rod and your staff,
they comfort me.

—PSALM 23:3–4

 For some reason, when I am in the midst of a crisis, I feel the need to clean. I want my house to be spotless, everything in its place. One Friday night just a few months after Audrey died, I decided that the playroom needed to be addressed. I told the girls what we were going to be doing, and I brought in the big black garbage bags. One was for trash and the other was for "the poor kids." We started sorting through old dress-up clothes, dried-up markers, and baby toys that I was holding onto. A couple of minutes into the process, Abby and Ellie began to discuss their plan of attack.

"Ellie, let's give these to the poor kids." Abby explained, "They LOVE naked Barbies with crazy hair." She waved around a ballerina Barbie that looked like she had spent a few hours in the spin cycle.

Excuse me?

"Okay. And also, let's give them this." Ellie held up a Ken doll with no head. Yes, I'm serious. "They will really want this guy." She shoved him into the bag and clapped her hands together like she was really starting to get somewhere.

(Insert "teachable moment" bell here.)

"Hey girls, I'm noticing that you are choosing the things that you don't like for the poor kids. That doesn't really make it a sacrifice. It just means you are giving them the things that you don't play with anymore."

They stared at me, wide-eyed, plan interrupted. I continued, "It doesn't mean as much if it doesn't hurt a little. I want you each to choose something that means something to you and then put it in the bag."

At this point, Ellie earnestly asked if I was going to put my new purse in the bag. I was tempted to make up a story about how poor kids don't really like Coach bags, but I decided to keep my mouth shut and let the Holy Spirit tell me what I needed to keep and what I needed to give away.

The idea of God doing this same kind of sorting inside of us has struck me many times when I am in the midst of "pruning seasons." Years ago, I was reading about the threshing floor in my Bible, and I became fascinated by it. Basically, it was a place high on a hill (so that the wind could assist the workers), where the chaff and the wheat were separated. The chaff, which was useless, blew away in the wind because of how light it was. The grain was heavier, so it fell to the ground and was gathered to be harvested.

God has brought this image to me many times in the midst of feeling "threshed." He has reminded me that His hands are doing the sorting. I beg Him to tell me what my offering should be, and then I ask for the strength to give it away. I guess you all know by now that my family has felt the sting of winnowing, and we have all asked many times why we have been chosen. That night after my teachable moment with my daughters, God led me into His Word, as He has many times, and promised me that if I would just spend time with Him there, He would reveal Himself to me.

I began to sort through all of the references to "the threshing floor" in the Bible, and I became more and more engaged with the way it showed up in beautiful stories that I have loved for years. The first is in Genesis 50:10–11, where Joseph and his brothers were mourning the death of their father, Israel (formerly Jacob). Later, Ruth went to the threshing floor and lay at the feet of Boaz at the command of her mother-in-law, begging to be "redeemed" by him (Ruth 3:6–9).

The story that stood out to me the most begins in 1 Chronicles 21:18–28, where David was purchasing a threshing floor from Ornan. Although Ornan told David that he would give it to him free of charge, David insisted on paying full price. He stood on the ground of "sifting" and explained that he would not take the easy way. He would do what was right in the eyes of the Lord, regardless of the price.

I will stand before the Lord one day, and I want to tell Him that I did the same. I want to say that I was sifted and that I did what David did at that threshing floor, because when I read these words that night, I knew I had started to uncover the beauty of what God was revealing to me.

"So David paid Ornan 600 shekels of gold by weight for the site. *And David built there an altar to the* Lord" (1 Chron. 21:25–26, emphasis mine).

He built an altar to worship the God who threshes.

And here is the best part.

"Then Solomon began *to build the house of the Lord* in Jerusalem on Mount Moriah, where the LORD had appeared to David his father, at the place that David had appointed, on the threshing floor of Ornan the Jebusite" (2 Chron. 3:1, emphasis mine).

The temple itself was built on a threshing floor. Oh, what beauty can come of the hurt! Although I have always known those words to be true, it was entirely different to read it in the midst of the winnowing. I needed to believe in the harvest that was up ahead and to trust that God would redeem the hurt.

Only God Himself knows why we each stand on the ground we're on, but there is something that you and I can do from here, and I choose to build an altar to the Lord. I'm not going to say that it is easy, nor that it is painless. It isn't. What I wanted on that night when I read about the threshing floor was for Audrey to be asleep in her crib. But she wasn't there.

And yet, I know this, and I am praying for you to also know it, deep down in a place where nothing has been for a long time. The God of Jacob, of Ruth, of David, of Solomon, and of you and me wants to help us build where the hurt has been. I am praying as I write these words that you will be inspired, even in the wake of devastation, to worship Him with eager expectation of the harvest.

Oh, Jesus, we know not the hour of redemption. Teach us to walk closely in step with You and to believe in what we cannot see from the threshing floor.

mending

— Don't give up on the threshing floor! The places that seem hollowed out and destroyed hold the potential for a beautiful transformation. We don't have the power to do it alone, though. We rely on the Lord for that. Where is the hurt right now? When you survey your life, where do you see the gap that feels threshed and whittled to the core? Do you believe that it isn't too late? I would love for you to meditate on this idea today, and to make a conscious effort to believe that the Lord makes ALL THINGS NEW. Glory be to God, it is never in vain. Don't do this alone. Call on the person/persons you have shared with throughout this book and ask him/her to pray this prayer over you:

— *Lord, we cannot begin to imagine how the world and our lives look different from your perspective. We commit _____ to you and tell you we believe you can make it beautiful. There is brokenness, yes, but not hopelessness. Make today's tears an offering that will water the soil for the harvest to come. Lord Jesus, bless us with the peace of Your unending love today. Amen.*

HUSH

The LORD your God is in your midst, a mighty one who will save;
he will rejoice over you with gladness; he will quiet you by his love;
he will exult over you with loud singing.

—ZEPHANIAH 3:17

 It was four o'clock in the morning, and like clockwork, Charlotte started screaming. Instead of her normal "please come get me and rock me back to sleep" sound, she was wailing. She went from dead asleep to sounding like she was desperately afraid in about four seconds. I opened my eyes and sat still for a second because sometimes she goes right back to sleep. Also, Todd is usually the one who gets up with her in the middle of the night.

"Mommy! Mommy! Moooommmyyyy!" I jumped up, because that was me she was calling. She wasn't just upset; she wanted me. Who can resist answering that call?

I jumped out of bed and walked toward Charlotte's room. Right as I turned the doorknob, she let out another piercing scream, so she didn't hear me walk in. We live in a house that has creaky doorknobs and pockets of the floor that you learn to step around if you're trying to be quiet. I know where they are. I didn't make a sound.

It surprised me that Charlotte wasn't standing up in her crib and bouncing, because she usually does that when she's upset.

I know . . . because I know her.

She was so worked up that she hadn't even noticed that I had gotten right up next to her crib and was actually leaning over the white wooden bars while she was flailing around. I could tell from her little wet head that she was sweaty. She was digging her fists into the mattress and rolling her legs around kicking the sides of the crib. She was more upset than I had seen her in awhile.

I prayed for her. I rebuked any attack of the enemy that might have been influencing her. I prayed for peace and for rest. I did it quickly, and I waited just a moment more.

She was still scared, still unaware of me.

Quietly, I started humming, "Hush little baby, don't you cry . . ." It was just enough to make my throat vibrate, too quiet for her to take notice, but she must have sensed something in her half-awake state, and she calmed a little. I started to reach over the crib, but I didn't want to wake her if she was going to go back to sleep. She didn't even need to know I was there; she just needed to feel my presence enough to know she wasn't alone. I kept watching her, though, and I noticed that although she was still upset, she wasn't looking at the door. She knew that one of us would come in and get her, but she cried to the corner, so distraught that she didn't lift her head.

And in the middle of the night, while the wind howled around Nashville and the rest of my babies slept, I wondered how many times I have done this.

I call Him, because I know His name.

And He answers, because He has always known mine.

When I am lost in the wreckage, trying to get my bearings, and while I can't even lift my head, He whispers throughout the madness . . . I am here, love. Rest.

I snuck in when you thought it was over, when you thought it was impossible. And while your back was turned and the world was upside down, I came near to you. I have seen you wrestle with your pain, shout in anger, and kick the sides of this life until the bruises reminded you that you could even feel at all. And somewhere, sometime—many times, in fact—I bowed beside you and sang. And when you thought you couldn't get to Me, I reminded you that I always, always come to you.

Hush little baby . . .

Charlotte stirred again, and I reached over and gently touched her back.

Hush.

She felt me, jumped up, and scrambled for my arms as if I might leave without her.

I never would, you know.

As she lowered her head into my neck, I started to settle into the rocking chair, and she was out before I even sat.

There were no words exchanged, just the truth that exists between a parent and a child in the middle of the night. And it says the same thing it always has.

You didn't know I was there, but it doesn't change the fact that I was. I heard you call Me and I came.

I sang over you, prayed over you, loved you from the shadows.

Hush, love. Hush. Another day is dawning soon, and we will meet here again, around the squeaky floors I have come to know so well. And when we do, you will remember why it is that you called Me in the first place, so long ago. And if you listen to the stillness, you will hear Me anywhere, anytime.

Hush.

Can you hear Him?

mending

— The first and most important word I want you to carry today is just this—hush. The noise of the world is deafening to a Christian if we don't remember His constant peace singing over us. We are never alone, never abandoned, and never forgotten. Not even in that place where you feel like everyone else has. Are you bruised from trying to kick your way out? He is watching you. You have no greater need in this moment than to listen for His voice above all the rest. All the while He has been calling you to Himself, and it's quite possible that the sound of your own wrestling is making it harder to hear Him. He has not left you to figure it out for yourself. He is a God who delights in you and desires your obedience, even in the small things. Today, focus on stillness and listening instead of grasping around in the dark. Trust in the peace He offers and grab hold of it as the lifeboat that will bring you to the shore of your desperation.

House of Mercy

". . . with God all things are possible."

—MATTHEW 19:26

I have long been fascinated by the questions that the Lord asks in the Bible. It started when I was reading through Genesis and I came to the part where Adam and Eve had sinned and then decided it would be a brilliant idea to run from Him.

Because God isn't really that great at finding people, you know. God asks, "Where are you?"

It's funny to me now because when I read it years ago for the first time, I thought maybe He was serious. Maybe He had added a little too much to the landscape and now He had gone and lost His very first man. *Or,* maybe He knew where they were the whole time due to the fact that He is the all-knowing, all-powerful God of the universe.

But why would He ask if He knew the answer?

It's the same reason I asked Kate if she had eaten her Halloween candy and watched her wide-eyed, chocolate-covered face shake side to side solemnly. She hadn't come to me, and instead I had found her out, clumsily assuming a few fig leaves (and hidden

Snickers wrappers) could prevent me from knowing of her actions. God is constantly asking us where we are, even while His eyes are fixed upon us. He wants our accountability, our recognition, our understanding of who we are compared to Him.

A couple of years ago I came across a story in the New Testament that affected both my prayer life and, over time, my view of God. Let's go a little deeper today because I want to walk you through this passage. If you have a Bible, look up John 5:2–9.

We see that Jesus was traveling through Jerusalem when He passed a pool of water called "Bethesda." In Hebrew, the word *Bedazzle* means "house of mercy" or "the flowing water." Many sick, crippled, blind, and diseased people sat beside the pool because it was believed that angels periodically came and stirred the water, causing it to cure the first person who entered.

There was one man there who had been an invalid for thirty-eight years. The Lord saw Him and asked, "Do you want to be healed?" (v. 6).

I would imagine he did. In fact, I would venture to guess that the Lord knew the answer to the question. I suspect that is not why He asked. Instead, I believe He wanted the man to hear his own answer.

Instead of saying yes, the man replied, "Sir, I have no one to put me into the pool when the water is stirred up, and while I am going another steps down before me" (v. 7).

Except, that's actually not what He asked. He asked if you wanted to be healed.

And guess what?

He asks me (and you) too.

Do you want to have a healthy pregnancy, Angie?

"Well, I do. But the thing is, I don't have a great track record, Lord. I mean, bedrest with the twins, then everything that happened with Audrey. I think the odds are against it. I mean, I want to, but . . . "

And gently, I hear Him whisper again.

Do you want a healthy pregnancy?

"Yes, Lord."

And that's what I should have said the first time. Because by saying yes to this question, I am showing that I have faith.

Do you want a strong marriage despite coming from a broken home? Do you want to raise your children to love the Lord even though you know they have seen you sin? Do you want to walk free from the pull of that sin that has plagued you for years?

Oh, the pool of water? It's not about the pool.

It has nothing to do with the stirring, and everything to do with the stirrer.

Which is exactly why He asks.

When Jesus hears my . . . oh, the man's doubtful answer, He tells him to be obedient and to disregard the pool. He doesn't need water, just obedience to the One who controls far more than just the water.

"Get up, take up your bed, and walk" (John 5:8).

So he did.

Now at this point I need to state the obvious. He may not heal you the way you want Him to. This story was very much on my mind when I was pregnant with Charlotte, just a couple years after we had lost Audrey. One night Abby and Ellie were discussing the fact that mommy was having a baby, and the most important question they asked was, "Will we get to bring this one home?"

What I told them was that I really hoped we would. I told them that this was the Lord's decision, but that we should pray that we will be able to. In the end, though, we will love Him no matter what He chooses. Believe it or not, they were satisfied with that, and in fact, so was I.

I've been sitting by the pool my whole life. I've relied on people, history, and myself for most of my years. I'm sick of complaining about the stirring and the people who are faster than I am, making excuses when things aren't going the way I want them to go.

He is in our midst, and if you love Him the way I hope you do, listen for Him in the stillness of night.

"Do you want to get well?"

In my mind, I hear Him asking it a little differently . . . *Do you believe I can make you well?*

Well, yes. Of course I do.

Do you trust Me to determine what that will look like?

I'm not relying on feeble statistics and human ability. My God is asking me a question and I will do the only thing I know how to do.

Kneel deep and nod yes, believing that He can handle the rest. After all, it's *His* house of mercy. *His* unending grace and love.

Whether it's been thirty-eight minutes or thirty-eight years you've been waiting, one thing is for sure. He is the same God now as He was in Jerusalem years ago.

So get up, friend.

It's time to walk.

mending

— What is an area in your life where you need to conscientiously acknowledge a desire to the Lord? Sometimes we wander around in our frustration and never even go to Him with our request. Does He know the desires of our hearts? Absolutely He does. But just as Jesus prayed to the Father, so are we to—daughter to Father. Are you waiting on the side of the pool for healing but haven't told Him? Maybe you have spent too many days talking about how it's hopeless or that you don't see a way out. Spend the day making a constant effort to communicate (in detail) your heart's desire for whatever area you feel you need to. Write it down if you need to. Be specific and give it all to Him. He is not a God who stands at a distance. Thank You, Lord, that you want to have relationship with us. Thank You for allowing us to have an honest conversation about the longings we have for healing. We thank You in advance for the way You will mend us.

THE GIFT GIVER

But for me it is good to be near God; I have made the Lord GOD
my refuge, that I may tell of all your works.

—PSALM 73:28

 On December 2, 2006, Abby and Ellie turned four. We decided that instead of a traditional birthday party, we would take an opportunity to teach them about sacrifice and generosity in a very concrete way. We asked guests to choose several items from a list instead of gifts for the girls. Then, at their party we packaged the items as a group and later sent them to an orphanage in Africa. Todd's parents are missionaries in Congo, and we thought that Abby and Ellie were at a level of understanding that would allow them to experience this as a true offering. It was an amazing night. The girls had so much fun while our house overflowed with friends and giving that I really don't think they noticed there were no gifts for them.

Fast-forward a few weeks from that birthday. It was almost Christmas Day, and we decided to do some last-minute shopping. As we walked around the upper floor of the mall, Abby and Ellie spotted Santa downstairs. They stared at him for a few minutes and then (much to our great surprise) announced that they would like to meet him. Todd and I stared at each other. Not only was there about an hour's wait, but they weren't exactly "camera ready." However, if they wanted to meet the man, we weren't going to stop them. Let me explain why this was such a big deal. They practically dissolved when the Chick-fil-A cow approached them with a balloon, and the Easter bunny at our local Easter egg hunt didn't make it closer than twenty feet from us before he started calculating therapy bills and backed away.

We got in line and immediately found ourselves in front of the mom that came prepared. Her son was decked out in a little corduroy jumper with a giant hand-sewn reindeer face on the chest and real jingle bells on his antlers. Every step we took, he jingled menacingly while I stared at my children's uncombed hair and ripped jeans.

Then, in my moment of feeling like the loser mom who didn't create a fashion statement for the occasion, Abby's voice broke out above the crowd as we practiced what they were going to say to Santa Claus.

"I am going to tell him that I don't want any toys. I want him to give mine to the poor kids instead." She stared at me intently, a girl who had made up her mind. My heart almost burst out of my chest.

She had redeemed me. I shot a glance at the mom behind me, confirming my new status as queen of the line.

I bet bell-boy doesn't care about the poor kids.

Smugly, I made my way through the line, pondering future Nobel Prizes and humanitarian work right up until the moment came to pass the red and gold rope. Abby had been practicing her speech under her breath while we waited, and now had it well-planned. We were ready.

"Next!"

At first, she hesitated. After a little prodding, she edged her way to the elf-lady and was escorted to the big chair. She climbed up and looked at us, starting to panic. Santa was trying to reassure her as he showed her his stash of candy canes and talked about Rudolph. She wasn't listening.

I could feel her anxiety as I encouraged her, "Abby, you practiced. Go ahead! Tell Santa what you want!"

She looked at me and did the thing with her mouth that means there are tears and screaming on the way. But then, she did the last thing I ever imagined. She raised herself up, taller than she probably felt, and she looked Santa dead in the eye. I was so proud. I remember thinking, "That's it, Abby. Don't give up now! You made it through the last hour and now is your chance to make a difference!"

I felt like you could hear a pin drop when her little voice finally spoke. My Abby. My sweet, giving, caring, ever compassionate and selfless . . .

"I want a pink tutu. And I want sparkle ballet shoes."

My jaw hit the floor. It was loud and it wasn't over.

"And I want the purple Barbie with the wings, and the movie about the dogs that can talk, and the tea set that is made of real china, and . . . "

Oh, those reindeer jingles. Now they were mocking me.

Truth be told, I don't remember the specific list of everything that she requested in her massive list to Santa. I am quite certain that Santa himself couldn't keep up. I remember a flash going off and paying about $40 for a picture that still hangs in our playroom, reminding me of that moment. I asked Abby why she had changed her mind at the last minute, and she said that she didn't know.

I have laughed as I've written this and recalled that moment. I have always thought of God as a director of sorts. He always knows what is going to come next, but in my human understanding, it's as though He must just pop a bag of popcorn every now and then and watch it unfold below Him like a great movie.

Here is what He taught me then and continues to teach me as I walk through the pieces of life. It is one thing to be waiting in line, lost in a sea of faces and noise, formulating a good plan for how you are going to do things when the moment of decision comes. *It is another thing altogether to be sitting on His lap.*

There are moments in all of our lives where it's not just talk, but we have to look Him in the face and rest in the chaos that He has chosen to be our story. We have to remember that we aren't that different from a four-year-old who realized that what her heart wanted in that moment didn't line up with the plan she had. There is something about sitting in the middle of a mall and asking Santa for toys that just makes sense. It makes sense the way that asking God for a healthy baby makes sense. In the way that asking Him to remove a struggle or temptation makes sense. It's His job. Miracles and protection have been His business for thousands of years.

There were many, many times when I was carrying Audrey that I cried out for mercy, not thinking about the implications of what this meant for my faith. I just wanted my baby. I want my baby. I want her breath and her heart and her fingernails. Forget the whole "bigger picture." I'm here with You, looking at You, and I know You can heal her. Do it. That's what I want.

Ultimately, this is not what the Lord chose for Audrey, but I feel peace in the sadness, knowing that is ways I won't understand, He will be glorified through it. I'm so grateful for a God who makes Himself small enough to listen to us and big enough to cover us with his grace, even men we don't understand His ways. Thank You for loving us this way, Lord.

mending

— It's a funny story, but I relate to it more than I care to admit. When the rubber meets the road, though, what I desire is to be a woman who really trusts in God's best for me. That doesn't always mean it turns out the way I want it to, or even the way it feels like would be right. What it means is that I surrender my will to a God whom I can fully trust. In your life right now, are you facing a situation where it seems that the will of God and your heart aren't lining up? Spend time praying that the Lord would align your heart with His intentions, that you would be able to rest in knowing that He isn't disregarding you. He has a plan that we can't see, and sometimes the best thing we can do is simply ask Him to extend His mercy as we walk in blindness. In order to do this, though, we have to trust that He is in control and that He is trustworthy. My prayer for you today is that the Lord will reveal Himself to you as both, and that you will genuinely make strides to believe Him above any other source.

BLINK

 It was about four years ago now, just a few months after we lost Audrey, and I was leaving Bible study with the girls. Abby and Ellie were buckling themselves in while Kate was playing in the grass by the car. I turned to her and told her to run to me and I would pick her up. Her eyes lit up and in true Kate fashion she took off full-force toward my open arms. I lifted her way above my head and kissed her sweet cheeks on the way down.

As I put her into her car seat, Ellie said to me, "Know what, Mommy? I really wish I had a camera, because that was a beautiful picture you just made."

It caught me off guard, because I didn't even realize she could see me from where she was sitting.

Without really thinking about my reply, I said, "You think so, honey? Well let's just blink our eyes and keep that one in our heads then."

I smiled at my three sweet daughters, and then Ellie and I looked at each other and blinked our eyes—another moment captured and held as a precious memory.

On the way home, I began to think about what she said, and I realized how often I see the world in photographs. I love to take pictures, and I suppose my mind has incorporated a little camera that allows me to freeze moments and store them away. I thought about having driven to the pool the week before. To get there I had to pass under some amazing trees that make a canopy over the road, only allowing bits and pieces of light to pass through. It was beautiful.

Blink.

I thought about the way it was when I saw Audrey for the first time, red hair and those sweet rosebud lips. No crying, but there was breath in her. There was life to be lived . . . I am so glad to meet you, sweet girl . . . stay with me for awhile . . .

Blink.

After a hard day of school as a teenager, my dad took me out in his old-fashioned convertible to talk and make sure I was okay. We drove to this field in the middle of nowhere that he had found a few weeks earlier. It was amazing, because as soon as the lights went off in the car, what seemed like millions of fireflies danced around us. I was completely mesmerized, and as the hot September night soaked into our skin, we watched them light up the darkness. I felt like God spoke to me in that moment. It is one of the earliest recollections I have of feeling His presence, and to this day, whenever I see fireflies I remember the way the old leather seats smelled as my father loved me enough to show me that life is beautiful even when it hurts.

Blink.

Me, in a veil I had dreamed of wearing my entire life, and a church full of people who were celebrating the way we loved each other. I was so nervous because I was sure I would trip and fall, but then the huge wooden doors swung open. I saw him, and I wanted to run to the end of the aisle.

Blink.

"It is very possible that your daughters will not survive. Now is the time to start praying."

Blink.

"4 pounds 11 ounces, and the other is 3 pounds 11 ounces! They are here and they are healthy!"

Blink.

Kate recites her Bible verse [A soft answer turns away wrath . . .] as "A soft answer turns away the rats." I spit my coke out all over the car and tell her she is brilliant and that I love her for being exactly who she is. The next morning she uses a less-than-desirable tone with her sister, and I ask her if she remembers the Scripture from the day before. She nods yes. I ask her to say it to me. She replies, "I think the Bible says I am going to time out." This time it was coffee.

Blink.

Abby, in the backseat of the car, eyes closed and hands in the air, worshipping with the music as she has seen me do a thousand times before.

Blink.

"Lord, I believe. Help my unbelief . . ."

Blink.

Todd surprises me at our wedding with a song he wrote for me. It is called "After the Rain," and it tells the story of how he knew he was supposed to marry me one day when he prayed during a ˙ ˙nderstorm, and moments later it just stopped with no warning.

Blink.

My brother-in-law Greg calls, and tells me he went to play golf. He says he cried on the way home because he realized he will never play golf with his son, Luke, who they lost to SIDS just weeks after we lost Audrey. I never mention the conversation to anyone, but the next day, Ellie draws a picture of Audrey and Luke. She says they are playing in heaven. I look closer and see something I have never seen her draw (because as far as I know, she has never heard of the game). I ask her what they are playing. "Golf," she says, and skips out of the room . . .

Blink.

Another little redhead. Despite the odds that my heart could love this way again. She stares at me from her crib, and I cry because I know that one day she will hear the story of her older sister and she will only know her in pictures. Sweet Charlotte.

Blink.

I don't even remember the punchline, but I threw my head back and laughed loudly enough to wake the baby. I pulled the sheets over my head and told Todd it was his fault I was laughing so he should go tend to her. He kissed me on the forehead and told me I was beautiful when I laughed. I realized we were mending.

Blink.

These moments and millions of others both in the past and yet to come are engraved in the beautiful book I am making in my head. As I drove home, thinking through this concept after Ellie's comment years ago, the Lord spoke to me with a perspective I did not have before He did.

Angie, sweet daughter of mine. You know, I do the same with you . . .

Blink.

I was speechless, as my spirit knew it was His voice even though it wasn't audible. I have choices, every second of the day, to serve my Lord. To honor Him with my speech and with my thoughts, with the way I love those around me, and the way I worship Him. Every moment, there is another opportunity to honor Him, and I want to use as many of them as He gives.

There are many, many pictures I want to rip up and hide . . . maybe you do too. But that shouldn't consume me. Rather, I want to focus on the beauty of this gift that the Lord has given.

It is the gift of this breath, this moment, this photograph. It is my offering, captured.

We need not dwell on the things we wish we had done differently, nor should we even give too much thought to what the future will look like. We need not worry about the complete picture, but rather the fact that we have this moment. Right now. And I want to make it count.

I am sitting cross-legged in an old chair, pouring out my heart to you, because above every other thing I can think of, I want these words to be a beautiful photograph for the Lord I love.

Blink.

In a few minutes, I will go find my children their dresses, and we will go to a cookout with friends. As I snap their sandals and brush their hair, I will tell them how I love them and how grateful I am to be their mommy.

Blink.

Todd came in to tell me about something he is reading, and I nodded absent mindedly as my thoughts drifted everywhere but his voice. No, I thought, I don't want it to look like that. I want to love deeply, and for him to know that I care about what he cares about. I want to show him that I am here to listen and that he matters to me.

Blink.

I met a woman who does not know about Jesus. She is broken, bruised, hurt, and alone. I want to show her the way He loves her, to inspire her to let me into the places she runs from. I want to make His name known. I want my life to be lifted up to Him, offered to Him, spilled out for Him.

Blink.

"She is gone . . ."

Blink.

A crown of thorns, piercing his sweat-drenched brow . . . oh, my sweet Savior . . .

Blink.

You refused the bitter wine but drank deep of the cup that would not pass.

Blink.

I see you there, Lord, and I will not turn from You. Not in my joy, not in my agony, not ever. Not ever. I will remember the scars, and the gracious Love that the world could not believe . . .

Blink.

I'm still here, Angie. Tucked away behind this trusty old camera. Now remember, you have this moment, child . . . That's it, turn your head a little more toward Me . . . Do you trust Me? A little more toward Me . . . there . . . perfect . . .

Blink.

mending

— There are no words for me to adequately describe how profoundly this entry affected me. The Voice that spoke to me as I realized the power of a moment to change everything. A phone call, a whisper, a car she didn't see coming. And none of these—not ONE—is missed by His eyes. We don't skate out of view and hope He catches up with us down the road. He is everpresent in every single breath, and while I wasn't designed to understand the mechanics of how that is possible, I can say that I am grateful for this spectacular love. Take a few moments and write down a few of your "blink" moments. They don't have to have been life-altering—just whatever comes to mind when you close your eyes. Maybe it's something you wish you could do differently or even a callous word you spoke this morning. There is something about putting pen to paper that brings fresh perspective. Once you have created your list, meditate on the fact that the Lord has been with you for every single one, and there is nothing He can't redeem for His glory. Resolve to be more attentive to the "blink" moments you encounter, and make a conscious effort to speak to the Lord as they come to you, recognizing His presence and His sovereignty in all of them.

Blessed Be the Name

Naked I came from my mother's womb,
and naked shall I return. The LORD gave, and the LORD
has taken away; blessed be the name of the LORD.

—JOB 1:21

December 2, 2002, was one of the best days of my life, no question.

Before I get to that incredible day, let me back up a bit. Todd and I were married on August 26, 2001 (just before the 9/11 terrorist attacks). We were shocked to find out three months later that we were expecting our first baby. I was only about seven or eight weeks along when I miscarried, but it was long enough to fall in love with the baby. I have vivid memories of standing in the bathroom of our little apartment brushing my hair and crying tears of joy because I was going to be someone's mommy. It wasn't meant to be. I wasn't where I am now with the Lord, and to be honest, I felt like I had been abandoned. I went to the library and checked out a book about miscarriage, crying and clinging to it every night. The following March, I was on the road with Todd in Maryland when I told him I thought I was pregnant again. It was late and he wasn't sure it was for real, so I went to the store and bought a test. When I got back to the hotel, I said, "You know if I'm pregnant, you are never going to forgive yourself for not coming to Walgreens with me." We laughed and I walked into the bathroom. Todd says I walked out about ten seconds later with a huge smile. He also said he should have gone to Walgreens.

We got home; I headed back to the library and checked out a book on being pregnant. I walked on eggshells for a few weeks waiting to see what would happen.

It felt like forever, but the time came for our first ultrasound. Todd and I were in the room full of anticipation and hope, staring at the screen to see a heartbeat. Susanna, the ultrasound technician, kept saying, "You see it, Todd? Right here." He looked confused. I told him he could tell us if he didn't see it; he didn't need to be embarrassed about it. He told us that he did see the heartbeat, but he was wondering what that other flickering was.

Susanna moved the ultrasound wand up a little on my tummy, and there they were. Two little heartbeats. I screamed.

We got home; I went back to the library (same check-out girl) and got a couple books on twins. She smiled at me and laughed.

"Quite a year you're having, honey!" She scanned the books and told me about her twin cousins, who, based on her description, are probably incarcerated by now. She thought it was hilarious. I thought I was going to vomit on the counter.

In late September, at almost twenty-five weeks along, I went to Alaska with Todd for some concerts. I felt uncomfortable, but I figured it was part of pregnancy, so I wasn't too concerned. When we got home, my doctor said he thought that even though everything was going well, he wanted to do another ultrasound just to be certain. I now know that was the whisper of God as I am convinced that we would not have Abby and Ellie today if he had not been obedient to this prompting. It was a terrible day. The sweet doctor started the scan, and instantly, his face dropped. He told us that something was wrong and I started shaking. I asked him if they were alive. Actually, I think I told him to tell me they were alive. I will never, never forget what he said.

"They are alive right now."

The supervisor came in and explained what was going on. Basically, my body was responding as though it was time to deliver. They barely let me stand up to go to the car. We went straight to the hospital. They told me I needed to check myself in and plan on being there until I delivered. One of the first nights I was there, a nurse came in and found me crying. I told her I wanted the truth about what they thought was going to happen to my babies. She was incredibly sweet, but she explained that they were both well under a pound, and on "the cusp of viability." I remember the words. I remember the smell of hospital soap. I remember that I already loved them so much that I fought every minute I could to have them.

It turned out to be a lot of minutes. Ten weeks to be exact.

I was on magnesium sulfate for three and a half weeks, which was nasty to say the least and caused some side effects that included some very odd hallucinations. Time passed so slowly. I was scared and depressed. And I think there's something else I should tell you about that time.

I hardly ever opened my Bible.

I believed in Him. The whole story. I loved Him, but I thought it wise to keep Him at arm's length in the event that He let me down. I hate that that is the truth and a part of my story. I wish I could go back and do it all differently, but I can't. Instead, I can rest in knowing that He pursued me even when I acted like a jilted bride. He wanted me when I didn't want Him. He taught me about Himself, even as I resisted loving Him in return. I am forever grateful for the tenderness He showed me during that time, as well as the grace He showed me when I came running back in repentance and sorrow.

At a few days short of thirty-five weeks, they had to send me home because my insurance wouldn't pay for me to be there anymore. A few days later they let me stop taking some of my medication and I went into labor. I pushed twice and Anna Elisabeth was welcomed into the world. Two minutes and one push later, Abigail Grace followed. At 4 pounds 11 ounces and 3 pounds 11 ounces respectively, they were really tiny. Abby wouldn't cry when she was born, so they whisked her away before I could see her. They brought Ellie to me, though. I squeezed her and kissed her and smelled her and just loved her completely.

Abby was in the NICU for almost three weeks, trying to get her weight up. She kept having "spells" where she would stop breathing and they would have to keep her for a few more days. Todd and I brought Ellie home, and about ten minutes after we set down her baby carrier, he left to go on his Christmas tour. I would nurse Ellie, pump, drive to the hospital, nurse Abby, pump, nurse Ellie, go home . . . and on and on. I felt so divided. My husband was gone, my baby was in the hospital, and Ellie was with me. I cried every night dreaming about when we would be together, praying Abby would be with us for Christmas, which she was.

In this life, we will have both. That much is certain.

There will be the IV poles, the divorce papers, the sound of dirt hitting a casket. We will have moments where we can't catch our breath and all the world seems wrong, and we can't help but wonder if He even cares.

On the other hand, there are days when the sun warms us just right and while dinner is cooking and the kids are laughing outside, we feel His great pleasure flush against us.

It is hard to type these words, because I have been a woman who has seen much of the brokenness that our sin-scarred world bears, and while I know this next part to be true, I don't believe it's easy.

Our response to Him should be the same, no matter the circumstance. Whether at a driveway lemonade stand or a funeral, He is still the same God. He is worthy of our praise at both, regardless of what it feels like.

I wish I could sit with you and help you process this, because it could sound callous and cold, but it is actually a truth of great beauty.

God remains.

Nothing about His nature changes, whether it is storming or bright. Will you rest in the idea that you were made to praise Him in either case? It won't be easy, but it is worth pursuing. He bought our freedom at great cost, and one way we can praise Him is to recognize His goodness even when it doesn't seem good to us.

Don't waste your struggle.[6] You serve a glorious God, and even in the broken shards of life, He is worth everything we can offer to Him.

mending

— It's a tough one, isn't it? In some sense it seems ridiculous to be praising the One who allowed the sadness to come. I constantly have to remind myself of two essential truths.

1. We don't see what He does. Our view is so limited that what we see as the end of the rope is only a fraction of His story. We cannot let our "reality" dictate what we believe about Him.
2. He is really who He says He is.

— Lest you think that is a small statement, go over it again and again in your mind until it begins to sink in. We aren't just throwing caution to the wind and hoping it's all going to turn out okay even when it feels like a disaster. We are, instead, choosing to believe that He is actively in control and that we believe Him. It isn't chaos, it isn't a jumbled mess of a plan that He is trying to piece together. It's His sovereign, spectacular love, spoken in ways we don't always understand. Let this day be a day when you consciously remember that. None of it was left to chance, and one day we will meet Him face to face. We won't remember the moments where we were broken and raw, and we will see the tapestry of love that only He could weave. Today, friend, we have that choice. Do you trust Him enough to believe it?

BAROS

Bear one another's burdens, and so fulfill the law of Christ.
—GALATIANS 6:2

It had been a really crummy week. Todd and I had both had a lot of traveling, busy schedules with the kids, and a lot going on in the lives of our friends. There came a point when I had to stop and think back to how to respond to those going through hard seasons.

I sat in a Starbucks and reflected back on years ago when so many people rallied around us during my pregnancy with Audrey. One of the most amazing gifts I received was the love of people who knew me only through the common bond of Christ. Through that bond, those women offered a part of themselves to me. In fact, many wrote me just to let me know that they had explicitly prayed for the Lord to allow them to carry a part of my burden. Wow!

I know without a shadow of a doubt that the Lord honored those requests, and as a result, my burden was lighter. To this day I can imagine the way He distributed that hurt to those who were willing, with the most beautiful part being that He received all the glory for their faithfulness.

This reflection came at a time when several of our friends were going through very difficult seasons in life and facing potentially life-altering circumstances. I am a fixer by nature, so of course I wanted to be there with the right words, suggestions, or solutions to make decisions clear and paths easy. Sometimes that is what we are called to do, but in this instance I had to pause and wonder if it was what was best. In my quiet time, the Lord led me through a few scriptures, and as always, a little bit of deeper study led to insight that blessed and instructed me.

Have you ever noticed that sometimes the Bible can seem contradictory? As I read Galatians 6:2 that morning, it seemed pretty clear that this "sharing of burdens" was important, "Bear one another's burdens, and so fulfill the law of Christ."

Okay. Got it.

But then, just a few verses later in Galatians 6:5, it says this: "For each will have to bear his own load."

Interesting. So what gives?

The Bible is not supposed to be intimidating. It should not make you afraid to dig further, or to seem like an academic, far away, untouchable instruction manual. It's one amazing story, and you are a part of it.

So, ladies, let's dig and learn about the story that defines us.

Why did the apostle Paul write that we are to carry one another's burdens and then just a few sentences later say that we are all supposed to carry our own loads?

As I read the passage, I asked myself the same question, so I went digging.

Here's what I discovered.

In verse 2, the Greek word being translated into English as "burdens" is *baros*, which means "heaviness, weight, burden, trouble."

Now onto verse 5. The Greek word translated in this passage as "load" is different. This word is *phortion*. The word *burden* is in it's definition, so at first glance it can seem as though it really could be a contradiction. However, when I dug down to the full meaning of the word, I discovered something interesting. The word *phortion* is also the same Greek word used in the passage that says, "For my yoke is easy, and my burden is light" (Matt. 11:30). So how does this all come together? Well, one of the most well-respected biblical scholars, W. E. Vine, put it this way,

> *The difference between phortion and baros is that photion refers simply to something to be borne without reference to its weight, but baros always suggests what is heavy or burdensome. Thus, Christ speaks of His "burden" (phortion) as "light," where baros would be inappropriate; but the "burden" of the transgressor is baros, "heavy."*[7]

Phortion is what we are called to carry as disciples of Christ. *Baros* is the type of weight that is only of this world—the difficulties that come from living in a fallen world as a fallen person and with fallen people. It includes a sense of weight that is burdensome. I know that weight, as do you. We feel it every day.

While we can't shoulder the burden of someone's walk with Christ, we can shoulder the earthly burdens put on our friends. And, not only could we do this, I really believe it's more than a suggestion.

Isn't that incredible? I hope that this accomplishes two things in you—to prompt you to dig into your Bible and also to encourage you to bear one another's burdens and so fulfill the law of Christ.

I am honored to share the load.

mending

— Who in your life could use some help carrying a load? Be intentional in your prayers and ask the Lord to reveal a person who could use you. It might be in physical ways, and it might just be the silent prayers for a stranger on the other side of the coffee shop. I have been the recipient often enough to know that these prayers are effective, and it makes me want to be on the other side more often. Once someone comes to mind, consider how you can engage in helping them. Do they need something tangible? Maybe something as simple as a meal or a letter. Possibly they just need to have a good heart-to-heart conversation, and you can reach out. We aren't supposed to live our lives in isolation, and the Lord so graciously provided us with community that we might glorify Him by building each other up.

HER, HERE

Then Jesus told his disciples, "If anyone would come after me, let him deny himself and take up his cross and follow me. For whoever would save his life will lose it, but whoever loses his life for my sake will find it. For what will it profit a man if he gains the whole world and forfeits his soul? Or what shall a man give in return for his soul?"

—MATTHEW 16:24–26

 I explained at the beginning of this journey of *Mended* that each entry was edited and adapted from blog posts I had written over the past four and a half years. With the exception of this entry, all of them were edited and shaped so that the context was not so, well, bloggish. Yet, as we approach the end of this journey, I want to share an entry with you that is almost exactly as I wrote it just over three years ago. It's a bit longer, so get comfy, grab a cup of tea, and let me set the stage.

I had just returned from a trip to India with Compassion International. While there, we had visited homes where babies were being saved because of the ministry that provided prenatal care. We had the opportunity to meet the children we sponsor and see a picture of redemptive work that left me undone.

Let me be clear, though. This book (or any others I've written or will write) would likely not exist and I would not have been on that trip to India if we had not lost our sweet Audrey. I began to blog right after we received her diagnosis and only did so to keep family and friends informed without needing to go through the exhausting task of repeating the latest reports over and over. I could never have imagined how God would use the blog medium to connect me with women all around the world who had walked through struggles both similar and different from mine, but who joined together around the common bond of wanting to be whole.

What did I want? More than to be whole, I wanted my sweet girl to live. I wanted to be able to braid her hair and paint her toenails. I wanted to teach her to read and listen to her sing "Jesus loves me." I wanted to referee drama between her and her sisters. I wanted to get to keep her.

But that wasn't His plan.

Once I knew we wouldn't get to keep her, my driving force was to make sure she had weight. That she counted. That her life marked this earth and, more importantly, marked the Kingdom of God. That the pain of losing her would not be the end of the story.

By His tremendous grace I believe He has answered that prayer and continues to do so. Each word I write in a book or speak on a platform is a testimony of Audrey's weight and the sustaining grace of our great God to redeem.

Don't get me wrong, though; there's never a second when I wouldn't rather have her. Never.

But it is with that understanding that I want to share the post I wrote after we returned from India—a trip I would not have been on if not for the loss of our precious redheaded girl who we loved a lifetime's worth in the two and a half hours we had with her.

What am I to do with what is remaining? This is the life He has given. What should be my focus? And what about you? Your path may be totally different from mine. Perhaps you've blissfully avoided any losses or struggles. Maybe your *lack* of brokenness is what defines you. No matter where you are, I believe there is a lesson for us in considering how to be *her, here*.

I haven't blogged much since I've been back because I have needed to spend some time with the Lord, dealing with one little word and what it was going to mean for me.

Reconciling.

Because in Kolkata, I was her. And here, I am me again.

They didn't know anything about me except that I had hands and that I was there to help. It was a breath of fresh air to be used by the Lord in this way. Everything that I have tied myself to in life became beautifully, naturally, and completely irrelevant.

And I want to be her.

Here.

I feel so burdened right now, and not many people have a place like this where they can come and speak freely, praying that those who read would hear her heart. I am going to write for a bit before I go to bed and ask the Lord to work with my exhaustion, because He has already made it clear that He will not bring sleep tonight if I don't write these words.

I just want to be her, here.

Do you?

I want to be the girl who walked into Mother Teresa's home for the dying, and despite the conditions, went over to a man who was probably hours from death and put her hands . . . His hands . . . on the fragile man's arm as he tried to speak. I liked who I was there because I was hands on flesh, heart lifted in prayer, silently begging for mercy on a stranger's behalf. When I finished, he pointed at the sky and looked at me as if to say, "I am going . . . " Oh Jesus, to know that he is with You now would bring me such unspeakable joy.

So how do we manage to combine the beautiful calling the Lord has on our lives while actually living our lives? I can't get back to Kolkata today, but I am desperate to touch the sick and calm the fearful. Do you ever feel like you want to make an impact but your life doesn't feel big enough? This isn't right thinking, but it is natural.

A little more than a month ago, I hadn't met the faces that taught me about her. This girl who lived inside of me and wanted to be better, not because of the accolades, but because of the most exquisite peace that came from going where He led me. Trusting Him relentlessly, with great joy.

And I liked her.

Yesterday I was in a funk, and as the trash guys came to get the trash, I reminded Todd to see what their favorite drinks were. In the summer, we leave out a cooler on Wednesdays for them, right by the trashcan. After shopping for the drink that each man wants, the kids help us put them in the cooler. Then they play until they hear the sound of metal coming down the road, at which point they hightail it to the front window so they can make sure the workers get their drinks.

I also love to order pizza if we have someone helping out around the house with broken cable wires or a malfunctioning appliance. I love to talk to them and make them feel at home. I didn't really think anyone had noticed, but the last time the cable guy came, Ellie disappeared for a few minutes and then popped her head around the door and gingerly set something down before nervously running back down the hall.

She was gone before I looked down to see the plate she had brought over for our "helper," full of plastic pizza slices and a wooden milk carton. She had also included one piece of plastic broccoli and a slice of delicious-looking decorative cake.

And I realized that in some ways, ways I may have deemed small before, I can be her, here.

And so can you, wherever you are.

I most feel the presence of the Lord when I am serving others, and my great desire is to glorify Him in doing so. It's easy to feel that when you are a bazillion miles away and the air is thick with desperation. But then you come home, and if you are like me, you have a pretty comfortable life.

I think one of my highest callings is to be a godly wife and mother, and that is what I try to focus on. But I also want to feel more like a "city on a hill" in my everyday life than I normally do.

Raise your hand if you feel that way too.

Good.

I'm not alone.

And also I'm so glad I'm the one who decides how many hands are up.

I have started to realize that while I don't know what God has for me in the future as far as traveling to other countries, I have a ministry in my own backyard, and I want to make the most of it. I bet you do too, and that's why I'm writing.

It might be something simple, like walking around the neighborhood with your kids on a prayer walk, as you pass each house, mention what you know of the family's needs and then stop and pray in front of their house. We do this sometimes, and it's awesome. It's not as awesome when your four-year-old yells to your forty-year-old single male neighbor, "Hey, Mr. Chris! Did you get a wife yet?"

We are supposed to look different than the rest of the world. We shouldn't be the ones that waiters dread because we don't tip after dinner, or the ones that roll our eyes when something is taking longer than we feel it should. Quite frankly, we just aren't that important.

We are supposed to be a refuge, an encouragement, a reflection of the One we serve. I know it isn't easy to do it all the time, and in fact, I think is pretty much impossible. But it doesn't mean that as you walk through your day, you shouldn't search for ways to do everything a little better. Talk to your boss with respect. Ask the girl at the coffee shop what her name is, and make a point of remembering it. Offer to help when no one has asked. Teach your children by example. Listen for what someone is really trying to say instead of what you want to hear.

I could go on and on, but I think you get the point. The reason I wanted to write this post is that I want to be inspired, and I want others to be as well.

Be her.

Here.

It's not about getting cozy and staying that way. It's about being a disciple. A follower of Christ. Follow Him. Burdens, brokenness, control-freak tendencies and all. Don't wait until you have achieved a level of perfection that only exists in your mind. Remember that He built His church on Peter. Faltering, foot-in-his-mouth, mistake-prone Peter.

I love that he used Peter to show us His wild love for the broken. You have unique opportunities placed before you by the same

God who restored Peter, and His heart for His people has never changed. What is He asking you to do today, wherever you are? How can you be her, here?

mending

— I know. The little things we do don't always seem to matter, and we think we have to be grand in our gestures of devotion in order for it to "count." The truth of the matter is, the impact comes from obedience—and in that case it doesn't matter what the scope is. You don't have to fly around the world and rescue orphans in order to bring the Lord glory. If that is your calling, than certainly be obedient to it, but it might be something on a smaller scale. And that is okay. In fact, it's more than okay. We all have "assignments," and we aren't being graded on how enormous they are. We do have a responsibility to be good stewards of the situations and people He has entrusted to us, and that needs to be our goal. How can you be obedient with what He has given you today in order to glorify Him? Take a few moments and write down a few examples. If you can't think of any, than pray that He will reveal them to you, and be sure He will. Praise the One who loves us through our iniquity and delights in our worship, however many times we have failed Him.

WHAT IS LEFT

And I am sure of this, that he who began a good work in you iwill bring it to completion at the day of Jesus Christ.

—PHILIPPIANS 1:6

 I sat down today with the intention of writing what was to be the last entry for this book. I had a clear time line, a well-defined objective, and a perfect spot at a coffeehouse with a warm latte. As far as writing goes, this is the setup you want. I even remembered my headphones, which is a rare miracle in and of itself.

But here's the thing about being a writer. Or anything, for that matter.

You can make a whole lot of plans, and it doesn't mean the words are going to come.

I sat for a good half hour just staring out the window, pressing a few keys, and then deleting. Several times. Actually, more than that.

I was so frustrated with myself because I needed to finish this and turn it in. But I was just, well, stuck. There may be a few tricks that more seasoned writers can rely on for this predicament, but I don't know them. I slumped over in my chair, took out my headphones, and considered packing up and writing an apology to my publisher because my brain had stopped working. Then it occurred to me that my brain wasn't completing sentences, so a written apology was sure to be tricky. I sipped my coffee, grabbed my sunglasses, and started to pack my epic failure day.

It isn't often that I feel absolutely certain the Holy Spirit is speaking to me in the very moment it occurs, but usually after a bit I realize He was whispering to me. This was exactly that moment.

There was a woman, probably my mother's age, and she was walking slowly with an elderly woman into the coffee shop. I took notice but didn't really think much of it. They walked past me and found a table right in front of me (Thank you for making yourself obvious, Lord. I'm sorry I can't take a hint). I happened to catch her helping the woman to sit down, and something about the slow, loving motion brought me to tears.

I found out a few moments later that the woman, Margery, was ninety years old and visiting her daughter. Her eyes danced with a lifetime of joy, and I didn't want to pull myself away from her. I also didn't want to be creepy. Such a fine line, hmm?

I came back to my computer and sat down. I opened it gingerly and tears flooded my vision.

I needed to see love to remember Love.

He provided it for me. In that sweet, honoring, slow gesture, a woman helped someone who had surely helped her many times before. The tenderness of it was breathtaking. While her daughter ordered her food, I studied the back of Margery's sweater, her neatly done curls, her painted fingernails shaking on the table. And I wondered . . .

Who had she been before this?

I don't know what to say other than in that moment, through the love of another woman, I remembered that we serve a God who loves us to the end of our days. Deeply, and with fond affection for our every step. He provides for us, and asks us to do the same for others. Not a moment of it was missed by Him, and I couldn't help but consider that although I only initially saw her profile, she was known wholly by the Lord. He saw her as a reckless teenager, as a blushing bride, as a new wife serving burnt toast to her husband. As a woman who buried him years later, lingering close to him as long as she could. He knew her moments of fear, her greatest life-wound, and the song that always brings her back to the days of her youth.

In this life, we often operate in silhouettes and profiles.

We take what our human eyes can see and we piece together an image, but we never know the full story. We aren't meant to.

I will never, never forget Margery.

I won't forget her blue eyes or the way she took my hand and told me I was freezing cold. I smiled and nodded—only later realizing how right she had been. She was alive with life. I was a writer, huddled in a corner, trying to grasp at words while my Creator looked on and smiled at my misguided attempts to pull it out of myself. That isn't the woman I want to be. I want to be alive with His power, filled to overflowing with His story breathing in me. So then, the question becomes not "Who was she?" but rather "Whose is she?"

I may have been a woman of recklessness, a woman who turned her heart away from the Lord in frustration, a woman who cried herself to sleep because of the grief she had caused someone else. All of these are true, and many, many more.

What remains of this mess I've made? Fragments? Sharp edges and the memories of what never was?

Certainly not.

But only because of Him.

He is the Master Artisan, and while I can't know how I deserve it all, He tells me it is so.

What is left, then?

This. Only this.

That we are His beloved. We are the bride of a Bridegroom who leaves nothing untouched by mercy.

Margery is farther down the aisle than I am, that is certain.

But my eyes are fixed on the One who waits for us both.

Are yours?

Lord Jesus, let my life bleed glory the way Yours did. Let me not become so consumed with my circumstances that I miss the divine moments You have allowed for me. May my days exalt only You, Lord. May every word in this book remind women that they are the recipients of a love so wild that the world can't understand it.

You rejoice over us. You take the pieces we have long forgotten—even the ones that have cut us deeply. And you lovingly place them one on another until all we know is that You are the builder and we are Yours.

What is left, then?

Yes.

The light that breaks through the shards of brokenness and makes the world bright with promise. The glimpse of forever that whispers gently . . . *I have mended you, love.*

Now go and tell the story of a love so beautiful that it broke in order for you to be rebuilt.

In His great, powerful mercy, He wants this for you. He doesn't want you to be a woman who is limping through life with a bruised heart, but rather, one whose eyes are lit with the anticipation of Him.

It won't be perfect. I've given up on that. And not a moment too soon.

What it will be is the feeble offering of a woman who has been spectacularly ruined by a love she can't understand. A woman who never thought she could be anything but a mess. A woman who learned the truth behind the sparkling eyes and the gentle love that desires her to be, well . . .

Mended.

And I pray the same for you.

FOUNDATIONAL PIECES

My Jesus

I would feel that I had done a great disservice to my readers if I didn't include an invitation to love the Lord Who walked with me through all the pieces and made my life whole. If you have read these words and they have made you curious about what great love has brought me here, I want to encourage you to seek counsel in the Bible and a local church to find out more about the Lord Jesus Christ. Without Him, there would be no words on the pages you have read, nor would there even have been a story. He is the light that conquers darkness and it is my belief that He wants to do the same in your life if He hasn't already.

If you feel ready to take that step of faith, the Bible tells us that we must confess with our mouths that Jesus is the Lord. Bow before Him, believing that He is the One and only Son of God, and He came to this earth to rescue sinners with His love, perfect life, and sacrifice. We must acknowledge that we are in bondage to our sin and can never be obedient to God on our own. In order to pay the penalty of our sin, Jesus was crucified on a cross. Three days later, in fulfillment of the Scriptures, He rose from the grave and is now seated at the right hand of the Father. He has done this so that you might believe and put your life in His hands, being forgiven for all your sins and shortcomings, pressing into the great, invisible God Who has every hair on your head counted and every breath determined.

When you have professed these things to Him, trusting in His perfection, you are invited to an eternity with Him in Heaven, where there will be no more hurt, sorrow, regret or suffering.

There will be His face, and His glory.

And I, for one, cannot wait to run to Him.

If this is a decision that you have decided to make, and *Mended* had anything to do with your choice, I would be honored to know. Please contact my publisher so that we can pray and celebrate your new life.

I am profoundly grateful for the chance to share the Gospel with you, and blessed to know that through this ministry He has given, my sweet daughter still speaks here.

And one day, in the blink of an eye, I will tell her so myself.

With much love and appreciation,
Angie

THE CANVAS

My father is a painter and he is incredibly talented. He is also a phenomenal writer, and I could go on and on about awards and things, but the bottom line is that he is just a man who has been gifted in many areas. I did not inherit the art gene as evidenced by my daughter, Abby's recent comment after she requested I draw her a bird, and then earnestly asked why I had drawn a dinosaur instead. My sister definitely got the art gene. She is so creative and it just spills out of her effortlessly. In fact, she has her own business where she hand-stretches canvases, and then primes them and all kinds of other things I don't understand because I specialize in Dino-birds.

About two or three years ago, my father pulled out an old easel and decided that after a long respite, he was going to start painting again. He bought all of the paints, the canvases, the whole bit. He read for hours about theories on color and different approaches to painting, and all the while the canvas sat blank on the easel. I teased him about it, asking when he was actually going to *do* something instead of reading about *how* to do it

One of the most common questions people ask me is how I got where I am with the Lord—how it is that I have this relationship with Him, and how they can do the same. I always hesitate to respond, not only because I don't see myself as the ideal Christian (do any of us?), but also because I needed for the words to be

God-breathed. Several years ago I decided that I wanted to get serious about my walk with the Lord. I wanted depth and conviction. I wanted real and tangible . . . I think, in essence, I wanted *a surefire plan on how to do this thing called Christianity.*

Sound familiar?

I decided I would start reading books that would *teach me* how to fall in love with God. The first was a book about how to really have communion with the Lord, a lot of which was about training your mind to be still. I quickly realized this is, umm, not my strong point. For example, I was reading on this topic while in the bathtub, with the TV on in the bedroom, as I painted my nails. Todd walked in and asked me what I was reading and I started giggling because it was kind of absurd to be multitasking while reading a book on being still. After I finished learning how to be still, I dug into about four dozen more. It became insatiable—this search for *how* to love Him, *how* to trust Him, *how* to live my life for Him. I would ask people how they did it, and I would go to concerts and feel moved, but still not "get it." I did everything I could think of to "trigger" the relationship.

When so many people started asking me the same question, I didn't know how to answer. It isn't my nature to give giant, complicated Biblical arguments or to make myself seem higher in understanding than others (quite simply, because that is not the way I see it at all). What I did want, desperately, was a way to communicate how I got here, because I love Who He is. But I wanted something *concrete* because that's the way my brain works.

I like tangible things that I can wrap my arms and my head around, and unfortunately, knowing Him and believing in Him don't really fall into these categories, so how exactly do you tell others to "Just dig in and trust?"

So, I have been meditating on what the Lord is revealing to me about how I first sought Him. I read every book (minus the Bible, mind you) on "knowing God."

I was extremely well-versed in *theory*, but completely lacking in *practice*.

And to be honest, *there was actually great appeal in leaving the canvas blank*. I could stare at it and imagine the masterpiece, without the opportunity to do it all wrong, or worse yet, find that the whole thing wasn't even real.

As I have let these thoughts rattle around in my brain, I realized that for a long, long time, I liked *the idea of Him* much more than the real Him. Many authors told me how they loved Him, and for a while that was as good, if not better, as me doing it myself. No risk. I could read about missionaries and see this amazing Savior, but not really have to invest in relationship with Him.

I just couldn't take the chance.

I loved Him from afar, through others. What beautiful potential, I would think.

So as the books piled up, the canvas remained blank.

I realized that the way I had teased my dad was exactly what God was trying to teach me about myself—I was far more comfortable reading than I was "painting." I'm not sure of the day or even what led to it, but one day I laid down all the beautiful words that people had given me and I let Him speak.

And I heard Him.

The Bible can be an intimidating, big, tissue-ish paged book to many. But when I opened it, I asked for Him to help it come alive for me and it didn't take long. I realized as I read through Genesis that what I had thought would be boring and dry was actually fascinating, and filled my mind with the kind of images that no other book could.

And so in a sense, I began to sketch.

Slowly, carefully, and with many eraser marks, the form of my love for the Lord began to take shape. As I grew in confidence, I pulled out dusty oil paints that allowed me to brighten it, and I started taking the time to fill in details here and there. On occasion, I have taken a step back from the easel and I have seen things I never knew I could paint. He has given me great courage in the darkest of nights, and intense joy in the least likely of places.

So how do I answer all of those e-mails, piled in an in-box, asking me how to make faith real?

Disregard the manuals that people have written and *pick up the brush.*

I am sitting in front of a computer screen that I have spent most of my life leaving blank, because I didn't think that I was really good enough to be a writer. I think about all of the canvases in my days that I have left untouched for fear of failure. Do you have any of those? The ones that you leave in "potential-land" because you can't bear to have them go wrong?

I think about the greatest masterpiece of all—the God I almost missed because I was so worried about the details.

So back to the question . . . how do *you* get there?

You won't find Him in a seventeenth-century book, nor will He be truly found in this book. He isn't found in the structure of a great sermon, or even a haunting worship song. These things can be amazing conduits that allow us to experience Him, and can help us to grow in our faith—but they cannot ever replace the one True God.

You will find Him *if you seek Him.* He promises us that.

Talk to Him, even if it feels crazy.

You will find Him in His Word.

Open the Bible and *read.* Ask Him to reveal Himself in the pages.

Listen for His voice.

Watch for the things He is trying to show you.

Dedicate yourself to seeking, and you will soon be swept off your feet by the greatest pursuer of all time.

Even if your hands tremble, pick up the brush and see what He has for you.

Have I mentioned that *my Father* is a great painter?

Well, *He is.*

I am praying that He speaks truth to your heart; the truth that no human mouth can convey, and no hands can quite capture in writing. I am praying that He makes Himself known to you, and that you fall deeply in love with Him. Head over heels, turn over your life and trust Him love. The kind that urges you to live with holy abandon.

NOTES

1. Sally Lloyd-Jones, *The Jesus Storybook Bible: Every Story Whispers His Name* (Grand Rapids: Zonderkidz, 2007), 304.

2. Ian Morgan Cron, *Chasing Francis: A Pilgrim's Tale* (Colorado Springs: NavPress, 2006), 67.

3. Ibid.

4. Beth Moore, *Esther: It's Tough Being a Woman* (Nashville: LifeWay Press, 2008).

5. Source unknown.

6. Pastor John Piper and Desiring God Ministries has a great series, "Don't Waste Your Cancer," that they wrote in the midst of his treatment for the illness. For anyone considering some really practical ways to conform your thinking in the midst of a struggle, it could be a really helpful resource. The pamphlet of the message is available for free download on the *Desiring God* Web site at http://www.desiringgod.org/resource-library/online-books/dont-waste-your-cancer.

7. W. E. Vine, *Reflections on Words of the New Testament* (Nashville: Thomas Nelson, 2011), 21–22.

ALSO FROM ANGIE SMITH

I Will Carry You
The Sacred Dance of Grief and Joy

Chapter 1 Sampler

Chapter 1
Us

*And the cup he brings, though it burn your lips,
has been fashioned of the clay which the Potter
has moistened with His own sacred tears.*
—Kahlil Gibran*

If there is one thing I have learned about raising three daughters, it is this: it is an unspoken law that if you are running late, you will not be able to find the sixth shoe.

It's life as a mommy. They are running in every direction, full of life: and all the while you are trying to rein them in and explain why Mrs. Adams won't understand if we are late for gymnastics again. Most of the time I just giggled and chased them around until I inevitably caved and let them wear mismatched shoes, imagining the looks of horror I would receive from the on-time moms.

Our biggest problems in life during the girls' younger years were things like finding the sixth shoe.

* I have been encouraged and ministered to by the words of various writers as I've gone through the grieving process. I am so thankful for the way the Lord has used their words in my life. However, quoting specific words from any author should not be understood to be an endorsement or sign of agreement with everything they have written.

I miss those days.

We made plans for forever, like you're supposed to do when you're a family. We were so in love with our life that it was impossible to consider anything else. Just love one another deeply and try to make each moment count for something. Run the race with joy, and it will all be OK.

How could we have known?

And even if we had, I can't say we would have done it any differently. We loved without abandon, each day and night filled with the hope and expectation that we would always be together. Whether nestled under a cozy quilt watching a movie or photographing the girls having a hose fight with the neighbor kids in the backyard, one thing was for sure . . .

We were a family, and everything was exactly as it should be.

My husband Todd sings in a Christian group called Selah, and when I look back at the way God started our family, I can't help but wonder how we managed to keep our sanity.

Just a few months after we were married, I was right in the middle of a conversation with Todd when it happened. I don't remember what we were talking about, but I do know I made a rather abrupt exit as I dashed to the bathroom with my hand over my mouth. I spent the next few hours assuming I had a nasty flu, but in the morning I realized the timing of this "flu" was a little suspicious. Todd ran to the store and bought our first of many pregnancy tests, and I watched as the little line told me I was going to be a mommy. We were completely shocked, but after about six more tests (anyone else done this?) with the same result, I figured it was really happening. I stared in the mirror as I got ready to go out that day, looking at my reflection and imagining what it was going to look like in the coming days.

I never got the chance to see that.

At around nine weeks I miscarried the baby, and I was devastated. Todd was sad, but he hadn't connected the way I had with the baby. His biggest concern was making sure I was OK. He was so tender with me as I tried to process the fact that there had been a life inside me that was gone.

That was the first time in our marriage that we had to walk through loss. We knew it wouldn't be our last, and that our vows included times like these, but it was hard. As a woman, I wondered if something was wrong with me. I would stay awake at night and wonder if I would ever have children. I had just finished a graduate degree in developmental psychology, and pretty much every decision I had made in my life revolved around my love for children. I couldn't help but wonder if motherhood wasn't going to happen the way I had always dreamed it would.

We were fortunate that the Lord didn't wait long to bless us again. I will never forget being out on the road with Todd, sensing that something was happening. It was eleven at night and I told him we needed to find a store that was open so I could take a pregnancy test. He covered his head with a pillow and laughed (mostly because I said this every month in the hopes that it would come up with the pretty pink line).

"Todd. We're in Maryland. You know how I am with finding my way around. What if I get lost?" He looked up at me with tired eyes, pleading with me to let it go.

"Honey, can we go in the morning? Let's get some sleep, and we can do it on the way out."

Clearly he did not understand the urgency of a woman in this mind-set.

"No, I can't wait. I have got to go now. There has to be something right around the corner." I grabbed the rental car keys and kissed him on the forehead.

He fell back on to the bed, knowing I wasn't going to budge.

"And Toddy? You are seriously going to regret not going with me if it turns out I'm pregnant." I smiled mischievously and closed the door behind me while he laughed.

I came back into the hotel room about a half hour later and ran straight for the bathroom. I watched as the colors changed immediately, clue number one to what we would later discover. Without even bothering to wait for it to make it all the way across the little screen, I opened the bathroom door and held the stick straight in front of me. I waited a second to make sure he was paying attention and then peeked my head out with a giant smile.

Todd sat straight up in bed, his eyes adjusting to the light and his mind adjusting to what was happening.

"Are you serious?"

I nodded.

I screamed with delight and jumped into bed, settling into my familiar spot on his chest.

He grabbed the test and stared at his future.

"Congratulations, Daddy."

In disbelief he set his hands on my stomach.

"Wow." It was about all he could manage.

"Yeah, wow."

We lay in silence for a few minutes, smiling in the darkness.

"Hey babe?" I asked.

"Yeah?"

"You totally should have come with me."

We laughed as we pulled the covers up, both of us in awe that God had chosen us.

And boy, had He ever.

⚬⟋⟋⟍⚬

After my initial miscarriage I had gone to the library down the street and checked out a book about pregnancy loss. The sweet librarian recognized me and acknowledged my pain as she scanned the book.

"God bless you, honey." She looked deep into my red eyes, ministering to me without another word.

I started to cry because it was such a simple gesture, and it meant more to me than I knew how to say to her.

After I got the positive test result, I was eager to go back and check out another book—this time, one on pregnancy. I saw the librarian working at the counter and waved. A few minutes later I set down three pregnancy books on the counter, and she clapped her hands in delight.

A few days later I went in for my twelve-week checkup, and they did an ultrasound.

After a rather shocking appointment, I made my way back to the library and smiled when I saw my library friend working. I watched her face light up as I set down a new set of books.

This time they were on parenting *twins*.

She looked up at me in total shock and started laughing.

"Oh, God bless you, honey! I'm sort of hopin' for your sake that I won't be seein' you tomorrow!"

❦

Aside from some discomfort, everything seemed to be going smoothly with my pregnancy, but my doctor suggested I have another ultrasound at around twenty-five weeks just to make sure. We knew we were having two girls and we were pretty set on names. At the end of August, we went in to have another look at the babies, and within about a minute we knew something was terribly wrong. The technician who was doing the ultrasound looked like he was in shock, and he got tears in his eyes as he told us he needed to get his supervisor. I felt like I couldn't breathe, and I asked him if they were alive.

"They are alive right now."

Those words will haunt me for the rest of my life.

His supervisor explained that I was dilated about three and a half centimeters, and that my body was threatening to go into labor. She told me I needed to get right to the hospital, and they called for a wheelchair as they weren't even comfortable with letting me stand up.

I sobbed the whole way over. My first night in the hospital a sweet nurse came in and sat with me, explaining that my babies were on "the cusp of viability," and that they were going to do everything they could to keep them inside me for as many weeks as possible. She was incredibly kind but also honest, and the truth was that it was an incredibly serious and unpredictable situation. A few days later I had surgery to try to prevent my cervix from opening any more. I continued to be on a round of the most horrific drugs known to man.

If you are familiar with magnesium sulfate, you understand. They had me on that one for three weeks. At one point I thought my

IV pole was a trick-or-treater. Todd was on the road, and my best friend Audra was with me, so at that point she told me she thought it would be a good idea to go to sleep.

After ten weeks of touch-and-go in the hospital, they felt I was in a safe zone and sent me home. They stopped one of my medications a few days later, and I started having contractions. I had a gloriously short and easy delivery, and on December 2, 2002, we welcomed Ellie and Abby into the world just two minutes apart. Weighing in at four pounds eleven ounces and three pounds eleven ounces respectively, they were tiny but perfect.

Abby was rushed to the NICU immediately, and we never heard her make a sound. She had a few complications with her breathing, but overall she did great. She was an itty-bitty thing, but she was a fighter!

We brought Ellie home from the hospital, set down her baby carrier, and I kissed Todd good-bye as he left for his Christmas tour. I will never forget those first few moments of silence after the door closed behind him. I stared at Ellie in her car seat and just began to weep. I was hormonal, alone, and in charge of two people's lives. I was scared stiff. I had one baby at home and the other in the NICU, and trying to nurse two babies on different schedules who were a half an hour away from each other was, to say the least, very difficult.

One night, when I felt like I had reached the end of myself, I walked into the NICU and heard a familiar sound. It took me a minute to put it together, and when I did, I asked what they were listening to. The nurse (who had no idea who my husband was) replied, "It's the new Selah Christmas CD, and it is so, so great."

I couldn't believe it.

"Do you listen to it a lot?" I asked.

Tears filled my eyes as I anticipated her answer.

"Oh yes, all the time. The babies love it."

I started crying because all this time, when I felt awful that Todd and I couldn't be there with her every moment, God had provided a way for her daddy to be singing over her. The nurses came to me and put their arms around me as I told them who I was and why this CD was so special to me. I remember one of the ladies reminding me that His ways are not our ways and we must believe even when we can't see the way out.

Abby made such great strides that our prayers were answered, and she came home just before Christmas. The high-risk doctor who treated me came into my room one day and, in a hushed tone, told me that my God had performed a miracle. He smiled as he left the room, and at that moment I had no idea that I would see him again a few years down the road in a much different situation.

Lights strung, presents wrapped, and two redheaded bundles that had defied the odds. Could life get any better? In the midst of it all, Todd and I fell in love with each other in a whole new way. We stayed up late at night and played cards in bed, covering each other's mouths to stifle laughter that might wake the babies. We realized the awesome responsibility we had been given and dove into it headfirst.

The peace of God settled into our tiny apartment every night as Todd sang lullabies and I gently rocked the girls to sleep. After sneaking out of their room (which was a closet!), we would play rock-paper-scissors to see who would feed which baby during the night.

The loser had to take Abby, who was notorious for waking up at least ten times during the night. When I would hear her stirring at 4:00 a.m., I would tickle Todd tauntingly and whisper, *"Your baby's up, hon. Have fun!"* He would roll over and whack me with a pillow. The next night we reversed roles. When I think about that time in our lives, I just remember laughter. I really understood what love was supposed to be and who I wanted to be as a mother. We were sleep deprived for sure, but we couldn't get enough of them. We lived in a hazy blur of joy and chaos, knowing that above all we were really in it together now.

A few months later I was dancing with Todd at a friend's wedding, his scruffy cheek pressed against mine as we swayed together in an unspoken promise: *This will never be taken from us.*

We came home from the wedding and ran up to see our sleeping beauties, sweaty headed and flushed with the joy of another full day. Their personalities were starting to take shape, and since we loved Louis Armstrong's "What a Wonderful World," we dubbed the pensive Ellie our "dark sacred night," and gregarious Abby our "bright blessed day." I tucked them deep into the safety of their covers, and the same implicit promise filled the room: *This will always be ours.*

What a wonderful world indeed.

What can I say? The twins were pretty much the perfect kids. They slept all the time, they ate whatever we fed them, they were even tempered, they smiled at strangers, and loved to snuggle. They were the kind of kids people fall in love with the moment they meet them. They wanted to help with everything around the house, cleaned up after themselves, played nicely with all their little friends, and constantly filled the house with the sound of joy.

I began to formulate a theory in my mind, which was based almost entirely on the fact that I must be the most perfect mother to ever grace the face of the earth. I smiled as people marveled at them sitting in the grocery carts while I shopped, and inwardly shook my head as we passed women with their unruly children. I nodded like royalty as women commented that they had never seen such well-behaved, sweet children. *Oh, why thank you. Really? Well, I guess we are just blessed to have such good girls. . . . You are too kind. . . . Oh, how sweet. . . .*

I have an image of God sitting in heaven, munching on a big bowl of popcorn as the days counted down to September 7, 2005.

cℐℴ

It was a perfectly planned (see where this is going?), crisp, fall afternoon when Sarah Katherine Smith came raging into the world about an hour and a half after I went into labor (yes, you read that correctly). She screamed like a wild animal in pain when they bathed her, smacked her way out of her newborn blanket, and stared at me with a look that said, "I'm going to need some more information here, lady." I heard a nurse make a comment under her breath about how I was going to have my hands full. I was not at all intimidated.

Clearly, I thought, *they did not know they were dealing with super mom.*

A few months passed, and I realized that the Lord, in His infinite (and often humorous) wisdom, had decided to give me the childhood version of myself to parent. I must say that the level of glowing satisfaction I have seen on my father's face in the past four years has approached sinful.

Kate is the most life-filled, passionate, willful blessing I have ever had the pleasure of raising. We always prayed that we would have a third child who wouldn't slip into the background and be overshadowed by the twins. When I was pregnant with her, I had horrible images of her sitting alone in the corner and feeling like a loner because she didn't have a partner the way they did. We prayed for her to have a voice, to have courage, to have strength, unwavering enthusiasm, determination, and conviction. In retrospect I think we may have overdone it a little.

Her enormous brown eyes and deep husky voice bring life into every room she enters. I see a lot of myself in her. You can't keep that girl from what she wants; one day, when she gets her arms around Jesus, she is going to take the world by storm. Until that day, I am drinking a lot of soothing tea and praying that I enter my late thirties with most of my hair.

When Kate was about two, we started talking about having another baby.

Let me restate that.

We had half a conversation and the stick turned pink.

Even from the beginning there was no question that this baby was supposed to be ours. We broke the news to the girls, who proceeded to request a boy who would not be interested in their toys. We told them we would do the best we could.

At about sixteen weeks we went in for a regular ultrasound, and we discovered that we were, much to the girl's chagrin, going to have another pair of sweet little girl hands digging in the Barbie bin. Other than that it was a normal ultrasound, although we did find out later that the technician had noted that there was less fluid than would be expected.

They suggested I have a follow-up ultrasound at around eighteen weeks just to make sure everything looked OK. We headed home with the thought that everything seemed to be all right. I had felt uneasy about this pregnancy from the beginning so it was nice to have a little reassurance. After my experience with Abby and Ellie, it was hard to ever feel totally at peace about being pregnant, but this was different. I felt so uneasy that I had trouble sleeping, and I Googled myself into every possible tragedy.

The kids actually took the gender announcement surprisingly well, and we moved into full swing nesting mode as a family. We took out one of the old cribs and set it up in Kate's room, which she was very pleased about because it meant graduation to a big-girl bed. We talked about names and all the fun things we were going to do with the new baby, and we stared at her ultrasound picture and dreamed of what life would be like with another car seat.

We decided to name her Audrey Caroline after my best friend Audra, with her middle name coming from mine (Carole). The girls were disappointed that we had eliminated "Shimmer," "Rainbow Flurry," and "Feather Dancer" so quickly. Thankfully they approved of Audrey, so it was agreed.

We were going to have another stocking hanging from the mantle next year.

One of my tests came back slightly abnormal, but my doctor wasn't worried because this particular test has an extremely high rate of false positives. He did suggest that I go ahead and have a follow-up ultrasound to see if the baby had Down syndrome. As someone who has worked with this population of children, I wasn't intimidated by the possibility of a special-needs child, but I did want to know so that I could start preparing the children and making every effort to make sure Todd and I were educated.

I was a little nervous about the ultrasound, because as mothers we can't help but imagine the worst-case scenario. I tried to keep myself calm, reminding myself that the Lord had our best interest in mind. He knew what we could handle, and we had to have faith in that. Still, I was uneasy about the appointment; I feared it was more serious than we were anticipating.

My mother-in-law was in town and sensed the Lord told her to stay with me for my appointment so she canceled her flight and decided to come with us. As we sat in the waiting room, we tried to make small talk, but we were so distracted. Something just wasn't right, and we knew it. A nurse emerged abruptly from the door behind us.

"Angie Smith." My stomach jumped.

"We'll be right back, Mom." I looked into the depths of her eyes, and I thought I saw a glimpse of fear.

"Everything will be fine," she said softly.

I kissed her cheek.

"Praying for you, hon." She squeezed my hand, and Todd and I disappeared into the corridors that now hold the worst memories of my life.

The enemy pursues me,
he crushes me to the ground;
he makes me dwell in darkness
like those long dead.
So my spirit grows faint within me;
my heart within me is dismayed.
Psalm 143:3–4

Yet I am always with you;
you hold me by my right hand.
You guide me with your counsel,
and afterward you will take me into glory.
Whom have I in heaven but you?
And earth has nothing I desire besides you.
My flesh and my heart may fail,
but God is the strength of my heart
and my portion forever.
Psalm 73:23–26

Also Available
by
Angie Smith

WHAT
WOMEN
FEAR

WALKING in FAITH that TRANSFORMS

ANGIE SMITH

978-0-8054-6429-0

Popular author and speaker Angie Smith
takes a personal and biblical look at the
dynamic emotion of fear and how to conquer
its negative impact on one's deeper faith.

{ Find out *more* at
BHWomen.com }

AngieSmithOnline.com

To learn more about Angie Smith's books, her blog, and her speaking events, check out AngieSmithOnline.com

Bring the Rain

Other Books To Consider

clothes shopping waste

7

stress media possessions food

an experimental mutiny against excess

Jen Hatmaker

amy e. spiegel

Letting Go of Perfect

Women, Expectations, and Authenticity

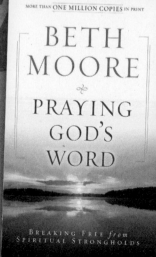

MORE THAN ONE MILLION COPIES IN PRINT

BETH MOORE

PRAYING GOD'S WORD

BREAKING FREE from SPIRITUAL STRONGHOLDS

7 - Jen Hatmaker
978-1-4336-7296-5

Letting Go of Perfect - Amy Spiegel
978-1-4336-7626-0

Praying God's Word - Beth Moore
978-0-8054-6433-7

{ Find out *more* at BHWomen.com }